INSTANT CREATION- NOT EVOLUTION

INSTANT CREATION- NOT EVOLUTION

DOROTHY ALLFORD, M.D.

STEIN AND DAY/*Publishers*/New York

First published in 1978

Copyright © 1978 by Dorothy Allford, M.D.

All rights reserved

Printed in the United States of America

Stein and Day/*Publishers*/Scarborough House, Briarcliff Manor, N.Y. 10510

Library of Congress Cataloging in Publication Data

Allford, Dorothy.
  Instant creation—not evolution.

  Bibliography: p. 190   Index: p. 199
    1. Creation. 2. Evolution. I. Title.
BS651.A52   577   77-8765
ISBN 0-8128-2159-9

To the loving memory of
my parents

Contents

Preface

This book is intended to present an entirely different viewpoint of the creation of man from the more commonly accepted "theory of evolution," which maintains that man evolved from lower forms of life. The scientific evidence that the evolutionists interpret in one way can also be shown to fit more precisely the opposite viewpoint—instant creation. Evidence can always bear investigation.

As a student in the public school system and in a state university, I was brainwashed with the theory of evolution. I was never given information by any teacher or professor about instant creation. This is still true of the educational system.

It is now time for students to be given the instant creation viewpoint.

1

Introduction

The purpose of this book is to call attention to the fact that the theory of evolution is just that—a viewpoint, full of flaws and errors. A further purpose is to present the theory of instant creation by an all-powerful, all-knowledgeable Creator as a viable and logical explanation of the origin of the universe, the earth, and the creatures of the earth.

The Theory of Evolution

Evolution is the theory that all forms of life developed from earlier forms, through a series of physical changes, with all forms being ultimately traced back to a simple, single-celled organism. The theory of evolution is not new. A Roman, Lucretius, wrote about this idea of the origin of life more than two thousand years ago, and so did the Greeks. The best-known advocate of evolution, and the one who has most completely defined it, is Charles Darwin.

Charles Darwin

In 1809, Charles Darwin was born in Shrewsbury, England. He first studied medicine and then theology at Cambridge;

however, Darwin was not really interested in attending theology lectures. Instead, he devoted much of his time to collecting seashore specimens washed in by the tide. Darwin was acquainted with Professor Henslow, a well-known botanist of the time, who is credited with having given Darwin systematic guidance into the natural sciences. Professor Henslow obtained a position for Darwin as the naturalist on the ship *Beagle* for a voyage that was mainly along the coast of South America. The publication of the scientific findings from the voyage made Darwin one of the leading "scientists" of the world.

By today's standards, Darwin could never be classified as a scientist. He was actually a naturalist. Darwin knew nothing about genetics; the discoveries of Mendel had not yet been published. More than likely, he knew nothing whatever about congenital abnormalities.

Darwin maintained that present-day forms of plants and animals developed slowly, over billions of years, from simpler forms. Those forms survived which best adapted to their environment through successive slight variations.

Darwin was a keen observer who, unfortunately, misinterpreted the facts. He was not keen enough to interpret the law of decay and death, which is so obvious. He should have looked more closely at the degeneration of the species.

Charles Lyell

Charles Lyell was born in Kinnordy, Scotland, in 1797. He attended Oxford University, after which he studied law and passed the bar. Lyell became the evangelist for the "uniformitarian" theory of geology, which James Hutton (1712-1797) had advocated. This theory proclaimed that only after extremely long periods of time and by gradual processes could present findings be interpreted.

A major flaw of this theory is that it does not allow for any world-wide catastrophic events (such as the Genesis flood or the shift of continents) to have taken place in the past. This misconception is still being taught despite the evidence which shows that world-wide catastrophic events have occurred.

Thomas Henry Huxley

In 1825, Thomas Huxley was born in Ealing, a suburb of London, into a middle-class family. His father was an assistant master in a preparatory school.

Most people think of Huxley as being a well-educated scientist and philosopher of his day. As a boy he read Hutton's *Geology,* Lyell's *Principles,* and Hamilton's *Logic.* He studied medicine at the Charing Cross Hospital and received a degree from the University of London. He was not interested in the healing aspect of medicine, but rather in the study of physiology.

Huxley is supposed to have coined the word "agnosticism," which means "the state of being without knowledge." In more ways than one Huxley was without knowledge.

Huxley was the evangelist for the theory of evolution. He gave lectures to the working class on the meaning of evolution. When Huxley was confronted with a churchman he would use wit and sarcasm to his advantage. Bishop Wilberforce, for example, who was not a scientist, was unable to counteract the erroneous conclusions of Huxley.

But Huxley was never as smart as he thought he was, and Ernst Haeckel was able to trick Huxley by his own falsifications.

Ernst Haeckel

Ernst Haeckel was born in Germany in 1834. He was the most outstanding "scientific" con man of all time. He was a professor at the University of Jena. Haeckel was not only the evangelist for the theory of evolution in Germany but for all of the continent of Europe. He added to the theory of evolution by his work on recapitulation in embryos. A later chapter shows how Haeckel deceived the scientific world.

Haeckel was an apostle of both "Darwinism" and deception. He proclaimed that there were intermediate fossil forms between apes and man. (More details of Haeckel's deception can be found in the book *God or Gorilla?* by McCann.)

Evolution as a Religion

To many people evolution is a religion. If it is a religion it is one with many false doctrines, teeming with errors and fables. The theory of evolution has destroyed the belief of many people in a Creator. This theory denies our rightful position as sons and daughters of the Creator. Many students are overwhelmed by the science and philosophy taught at the colleges and universities where, under the name of science, many false dogmas are taught.

Louis More has said:

> Our faith in the idea of evolution depends on our reluctance to accept the antagonistic doctrine of special creation, because this view of creation is foreign to our belief in the continuity of law and order.

This evolutionist is not aware of the process of degeneration, the second law of thermodynamics. See the chapter on Decay and Death.

The Beginning

When the work of creation was completed as recorded in Chapters 1 and 2 of Genesis, it was very beautiful. The surface of the earth was diversified, with mountains, hills, and plains interspersed with rivers and lakes. The sharp, rugged edges of the earth's surface, which we see in the mountains and canyons of today, were not present in the beginning. (Some of the barren rocks that we see strewn about are results of the Flood.) There were graceful shrubs and delicate flowers to greet the eye at every turn; there were giant trees of majestic heights. The air was clean and untainted by any foul odor from machines, animals, or man. The landscape was not only beautiful but peaceful.

Life on earth and the creation of our solar system took a very short period of time. The six-day time period for creation can be spoken of as "instant creation" when compared to the four to five billions of years the evolutionists claim that it took for us to reach our present state.

The Earth was teeming with animal and vegetable life brought into existence by the Creator, whose crowning work was His creation of man—male and female—in the image of Himself. In man's own realm he was to be a symbol of his Creator—living right, showing love, and feeling compassion and mercy.

Moses clearly sets forth the origin of man. It is difficult to try to reason how man evolved and developed some of his talents. Adam came forth from the Creator's hand having the capacity to become a musician, singer, mathematician, engineer, architect, scientist, or artist. Man has many attributes not possessed by the animal kingdom.

One evolutionist said on television, while being interviewed about a book he had written, that the same mind that man developed for hunting and killing was capable of building highly complex computers. This evolutionist seemed to forget that lions and tigers hunt and kill, but cannot build computers. God created man's mind different from animals'.

Man was placed as the Creator's representative over the lower forms of creation. The animal kingdom is not capable of understanding and acknowledging the sovereignty of the Creator, but man is. These lower forms of creation are capable of loving and serving man. Anyone who has owned a dog knows how much dogs can love their human masters. Many a dog has saved a human life from attack by an assailant. The Creator has put the capacity to love man within dogs. Even in the face of death, dogs have a loving obedience toward their masters. (And pet dogs serve as companions who never find and point out our faults as human companions often do.)

Rebellious men are so intent upon excluding the Creator from his original sovereignty that they degrade themselves by denying their very origin. When man came forth from the Creator's hand, he was of lofty stature and of perfect symmetry. His countenance was that of peace and health. Adam bore the Creator's image, both in outward appearance and in character. Man's mind was capable of comprehending divine things. His affections were pure and his appetites and passions were under the control of reason.

Someone may be asked the question, why is it, if we are made in the image of the Creator, that some of us are so ugly? Lawbreaking can cause ugliness. How? In many ways. For example, I have seen patients whose faces have been cut up and beaten to a pulp because they have broken the law by getting into drunken brawls. Also, ugliness can result from genetic inherited defects of the face and body. This topic is discussed more fully elsewhere.

In the Garden of Eden the first marriage was celebrated. This holy institution was originated by the Creator of the universe. Marriage is the first gift of the Creator to man, and it is one of the two institutions that, after the Fall, Adam brought forth with him beyond the gates of the Garden.

Another token of the Creator's love for Adam and Eve is that He planted a garden east of Eden and placed the holy pair in the garden. This was to be their home. In the midst of the garden was planted the Tree of Life. After the creation was completed, the Creator saw that everything He had made was very good. Adam and Eve were permitted to eat from the Tree of Life. (The disobedience of mankind had not yet marred the Creator's new creation.)

The care of the Garden of Eden was committed to Adam and Eve; they were to dress it and to keep it. Work was appointed to man to occupy his mind, to strengthen his body, and to develop all his faculties. The work was not wearisome like much of mankind's toil in factories of today. Our first parents had a beautiful garden that did not need fertilizer and sprays, and had no diseased plants.

The happy pair saw only peace and contentment among the animals and birds of the air.

It is clearly stated by Moses, in Genesis, that after the Creator completed the works of creation He rested on the seventh day and blessed this Sabbath day as a memorial of His creative power. This was the second institution that man was to take with him from the Garden after his Fall.

Adam and Eve were not placed beyond the possibility of wrongdoing. They were instructed about the rebellion in heaven, which had already taken place against the Creator. They were exposed to the rebellion but were given their choice of paths to follow. The Creator clearly indicated that the Tree of Knowledge, which was also in the midst of the Garden, was not to be eaten. Adam and Eve were not hungry, they had fruits, grains, and nuts so there was no actual need to eat from the Tree of Knowledge of good and evil. The Creator's only restriction, as far as eating was concerned, was that they were not to eat of the Tree of Knowledge. Disobedience to this plain, simple instruction permitted lawlessness to enter the world, followed by the woes of crime, disease, war, hatred, and sorrow. Eating from this Tree of Knowledge meant comprehension of what disobedience would bring.

The Creator clearly indicated to Adam and Eve that it was their choice whether to obey or disobey. They were warned that as soon as they ate of the Tree of Knowledge death would ensue.

The Creator made man upright, and endowed with intellectual powers possessed by no man living today. Modern man's intellect, in comparison to Adam's, would have to be considered greatly inferior.

One wonders why it is so difficult to believe that it took the Creator only one day to create man. Man and woman normally produce a human child in nine months. Now consider, if man in his realm can produce a baby in nine months, then why can't the Creator produce a man and woman in one day? The interval of time from conception to birth (then on to adulthood) is instant creation in a modified slow-motion form.

The Fall

Our first parents were warned against rebellion and the sorrow which would follow. The Tree of Knowledge was to be their test of obedience to their Creator. Our first parents were to serve their Maker in trust and love—it is not in the nature of the Creator to force anyone to love and obey Him.

After eating of the forbidden fruit, the first man and woman felt guilty and were in a state of anxiety, Genesis 3 reveals. Anxiety is defined as painful concern about the future, and our first parents had ample reason to be concerned about their future. They expressed their fear by hiding from their Creator.

There is a close relationship between the mind and body. If one is affected, the other sympathizes. We know that grief, anxiety, discontent, and guilt all tend to break down the life forces and bring on decay and death.

Clinically, patients who suffer from anxiety and fear have varying degrees of palpitation, tachycardia, sweating, headache, chest pain, gastrointestinal complaints, fatigue, and insomnia.

It is no secret that the emotions have a very distinct and recognizable effect on the gastrointestinal system. Some of us suffer only mild symptoms during periods of anxiety, i.e., butterflies in the stomach. But anxiety can produce hyperactivity of the gastrointestinal tract, which is, in turn, the prelude to pyloric and duodenal ulcers. Here we can see the deleterious effects of anxiety-producing disobedience.

The Tree of Life

It is clearly stated (Genesis 3:22) that if man continued to eat of the Tree of Life, which was in the garden east of Eden, he would continue to live. The question now arises, did the fruit of the Tree of Life contain some kind of supervitamin or vitamins that would prevent aging, decay, and death? The word "vitamin" comes from *vita,* meaning "life." Thus, the fruit of the Tree of Life must have contained some type of vitamin or vitamins that were essential for continuing life.

Let us consider for a moment thiamine (Vitamin B_1), which is essential for life. Avitaminosis of thiamine will cause beriberi.

This vitamin's enzymatic function is essential for the proper metabolism of carbohydrates and fats. The clinical manifestations of beriberi are vomiting, respiratory difficulty, cyanosis, tachycardia, hypotension, and convulsions. In some cases there may even be congestive heart failure. Thiamine deficiencies are rarely seen in this country except in alcoholics and recluses and others who eat highly refined or overcooked food. These patients respond very well to B-complex therapy.

A thiamine deficiency is essentially a pyruvic-acid intoxication, which affects all tissues and organs. Death can actually ensue from a thiamine deficiency. Therefore, it is scientifically possible that a supervitamin was in the fruit of the Tree of Life and would prevent the aging process.

It is not difficult for a physician to understand that the cause of Adam and Eve's fall was appetite, as this is the most prevailing character defect of mankind today. We are very oral-oriented creatures. Man's perverted appetite is manifested by overindulgence not only in food, but also in drugs, alcohol, and tobacco.

The old cliché "Nobody is perfect" is certainly true. Although some evolutionists will argue that man is essentially good, this is obviously untrue, because the world is so bad. Who makes the world bad? It is the entire human race—human beings are bent toward evil.

It is beyond the scope of this book to discuss fully the Creator's plan for the restoration of mankind. The regeneration of man is evident in persons who have changed their characters by a supernatural power. Vicious criminals have actually turned into law-abiding citizens.

Conscience

What is conscience? Conscience is the innermost thought process for deciding what is morally wrong or right. The conscience has been called the watchdog of the soul. It can be called the traffic light of moral behavior—it tells us when to go ahead or when to stop. The conscience can also flash danger signals to us to be on guard.

Conscience is unique to man. Some evolutionists have attempted to prove that animals have a conscience. They claim that a dog or cat, when caught taking something from a table, will shrink because of being "conscience smitten." This is not the case. An animal learns from the voice inflection of the master when it is a "bad dog!"

The conscience has to be educated as to what is right and what is wrong. For instance, one culture may accept stealing as a way of life, while in another society it may not be tolerated. A child must be taught the ways of its culture.

What physical reactions are associated with conscience? When there is a feeling of guilt and shame, a person's body posture is less erect and his step has less spring in it. No one would question the obvious changes in a patient's posture and gait after a stroke. And the alert physician can see the same kinds of noticeable changes in a patient when he is suffering from a guilty conscience. One vivid example of such a patient is a teenager who had left my office after a routine checkup. My office nurse and I discussed the boy's physical attitude, which revealed a sense of shame and guilt. About one week later, we read in the paper that the boy had been picked up for burglarizing homes. I deeply regretted that I had not asked him if he was in some difficulty.

The conscience is also an emergency control over one's self-behavior; either a self-restraining (punishment) or a self-prodding (reward) mechanism that enables a person to adapt to society's demands. The cultural rules of society are transmitted to a child by parental authority, which is enforced by reward and punishment. The child restrains himself from forbidden behavior because of his fear of punishment. This carries over into adulthood, and the adult conforms to society's rules.

But this is not the entire meaning of conscience. Sometimes standing up for a principle may bring an individual into conflict with a portion of society. For instance, it takes real stamina to stand up for a moral conviction that most of society terms "square." What is now termed the "new morality" is nothing more than the old immorality.

The animal kingdom acts upon a locked-in behavior called instinct, but man is controlled by his reasoning power. Instinct will be discussed more fully elsewhere.

Sometimes temptation overrules conscience and the fear of detection and punishment, and a person breaks the law. This disobedience causes a guilty conscience and a loss of self-respect and self-pride.

When the conscience is continually violated, a person's mind becomes hardened. Alexander MacLaren describes this process of the hardening of the conscience in the following words:

> An old historian says about the Roman Armies that marched through a country, burning and destroying every living thing, "They made it a solitude, and they called it peace," and so do men with their consciences. They stifle them, fear them, forcibly silence them, somehow or other; and then, when there is a dread stillness in its heart, broken by no voice of either approbation or blame, but doleful, like the unnatural quiet of a deserted city, then they say it is peace.

We see this deadening of the conscience happening to millions, and it is reflected in the ever-increasing crime rate in America. My own observation is that people who use illicit drugs have hardened consciences and are deadening their sensibility to wrongdoing. They are in a stuporous state, which they call peace, but are unaware of the real peace they could have if they obeyed the law. A former addict told me that being "clean" gave him self-respect, and respect for policemen, whom he once hated and feared.

Human beings all over the world will go to great lengths to clear their guilty consciences. Depending on their religious culture, people with guilty consciences make pilgrimages to holy cities, bathe themselves in the Ganges River, and will do almost anything to atone for their misdeeds. It is fortunate that the Judeo-Christian concept of dealing with guilt provides for the person to confess to the Creator, who then forgives and bestows on the individual an inward peace.

The Scopes Trial

When an evolutionist is confronted with the instant creation viewpoint, he immediately heaps ridicule and scorn upon anyone who dares to question him. One evolutionist, in anger, questioned sarcastically, "Didn't we settle this forty years ago in the Scopes trial?"

No, we did not. All the facts were not in when this trial took place in 1925. Let us look at this famous "monkey trial."

Early in 1925, the Tennessee legislature passed a law forbidding the teaching of any theory that denied the story of the Divine creation of man as taught in the Bible, including the teaching that man is descended from the lower forms of animals. John T. Scopes was arrested for breaking this law. He was a high school teacher of biology in Dayton, Tennessee. It should be noted here that before John Scopes's death, he admitted on national television that he never actually taught the theory of evolution, but an arrangement had been made for him to be arrested so this law could be tested. The Scopes trial attracted world-wide attention.

The prosecution was conducted by the Attorney General of the State of Tennessee, assisted by William Jennings Bryan. Scopes was defended by Clarence S. Darrow, Dudley F. Malone, and Arthur G. Hayes.

Clarence Seward Darrow

Clarence Darrow, a brilliant trial lawyer, was the defense attorney for John Scopes in the so-called monkey trial. Darrow was a well-known criminal lawyer, whose chief fame came from being a "labor lawyer." Darrow was known for his great enthusiasm in fighting legal battles for organized labor. He was the defense attorney for Loeb and Leopold in their 1924 trial for murder in the famous Bobby Frank case. He traveled throughout the country debating social issues with noted opponents. Darrow, as an author, is perhaps best known for his book *Crime, Its Cause and Treatment.*

William Jennings Bryan

William Jennings Bryan was born in 1860 and died in 1925, a few days after he had won the Scopes trial in Dayton, Tennessee. Although he was depicted as somewhat of a nitwit in the movie version of the trial, this man was a noted orator and statesman. He served in the United States House of Representatives from 1891 to 1895, and was a delegate to the Democratic National Convention in Chicago in 1896. At the Convention, he delivered a very dramatic and stirring speech, which resulted in his nomination for the Presidency; however, he was defeated by William McKinley. He was only thirty-six years old at that time.

Because of Bryan's religious beliefs, including his disbelief in the theory of evolution, he was the prosecuting attorney in John Scopes's trial.

Bryan's books included *In His Image, Famous Figures of the Old Testament, Seven Questions in Dispute,* and *Memoirs.*

During the trial, Bryan was pictured as an almost fanatical religious crusader by the national press. Since most of the press were evolutionists, Darrow appeared to be the favorite. Bryan had been denying evolution since the beginning of his career and was well aware of the impact evolution had made upon the minds of American college youth. Of those entering college, only 15 percent were unbelievers, but by graduation time, this figure had risen to more than 40 percent. Bryan objected to the teaching of evolution as a *fact*.

Before the trial began, John Scopes went to New York and met with the officials of the American Civil Liberties Union. Clarence Darrow offered to defend Scopes without a fee, and Scopes chose him as his defense attorney. His choice was a good one; Darrow made a monkey out of Bryan in court.

While Scopes was in New York, he met Dr. Henry Fairfield Osborn, the President of the American Museum of Natural History, a well-known paleontologist and an authority on evolution. (When Osborn learned of Bryan's crusade against evolution, he invited Bryan to the American Museum to see for himself the "evidence" supporting evolution. Bryan declined Osborn's offer.) Osborn explained to Scopes that he was unable to go to Dayton for the trial because of his wife's illness and offered to get a testimonial letter from Major Leonard Darwin, a son of the great Charles Darwin.

In his letter to Scopes, Major Darwin wrote that he had great sympathy for Scopes's courageous effort to maintain the right to teach well-established scientific theories and to state that that which is true cannot be irreligious.

During the trial, Darrow dramatically implied that all fundamentalists are against anyone who thinks, and that Scopes was put on trial because of ignorance and bigotry. Darrow went on to state that he knew of nothing that caused more bitterness, hatred, and cruelty in the world than religion. He did note that religion had given consolation to millions. Darrow raised this question, "Can a legislative body say you can't read a book or take a lesson, or make a talk on science until you first find out whether you are saying anything against Genesis?" He stated that anyone had the right to investigate the evidence put forth by science.

It was evident from the beginning of the trial that Bryan was in grave difficulty. He was not a scientist, and did not have the scientific facts we have today. Bryan made the fatal mistake of taking the witness stand himself, and Darrow pounced upon him with ridicule and scorn. Bryan was made the villain of the trial; however, he won the case. The jury found Scopes guilty and he was fined $100.

Two years after the trial, the Tennessee State Appellate Court reviewed the case and reversed the verdict, thus preventing an appeal to the United States Supreme Court.

The results of Darrow's brilliant defense in the great monkey trial influenced the repeal of similar anti-evolution legislation in other states.

It is obvious that the trial supplied a strong impetus to individuals and organizations engaged in opposing and debunking the idea of instant creation. The final results of the Scopes trial gave great encouragement and added importance to the cause of evolution. Defenseless young students could now be taught, with legal sanction, the "ultimate truth" that man evolved from lower forms of life.

Today we have much more scientific evidence than was available when the trial was held in 1925 and can submit new facts to support our position that evolution is scientifically impossible. Therefore, let us continue to question all the evidence that evolutionists claim they have found to show that man has ascended from lower forms of life.

2

Errors and Myths of the Theory of Evolution

The Erect Posture in Man

One of the arguments used by evolutionists to support their position is that humans experience many difficulties, aches, and pains related to the back because they were never intended to stand erect, but were meant to travel on all-fours.

An aching back is a popular complaint—it seems to be in vogue—of not only the President or the educated and sophisticated, but also of the laborer as well. Orthopedic appliances are sold by the thousands. Some mattress manufacturers advertise that they specialize in making their products more comfortable for people with aching backs.

Drug companies are also in the act. One drug company, in its advertising in physicians' journals, pictured the skeleton of a human in an upright position superimposed over the skeleton of a four-legged animal. The ad suggested that man's evolution to the upright position had made him more vulnerable to backaches. This doctrine is taught by evolutionists to medical and nursing students.

▷ Let's examine the facts. Is the aching back only experienced by man? Do animals who travel on four legs suffer from back problems? What do veterinarians say about the back problems of animals?

Intervertebral disc protrusion in animals has been a known fact in veterinary medicine for many years. Some breeds of dogs seem to have a predisposition toward this disease. The Dachshund, Beagle, and Pekingese seem to be more commonly affected than other breeds.

Comparative anatomy involving the vertebra and the disc is similar in man and in the dog. The discs between the vertebrae act as cushions for weight bearing. They are composed of an intermass of gelatinous material, with an outer laminated fibrous ring. These discs prevent wear and tear of the vertebral joint spaces, as they are uniquely designed to serve as an elastic cushion between the bony vertebral surfaces; they allow movement but minimize trauma and shock. Their elasticity allows for compression. These discs are the shock absorbers to the intervertebral joints.

Frequently, the complaints are similar for both man and animal at the onset of a herniated disc. I recall one patient stating that he had never had an ache in his back until he jumped off a truck. A cat that never had any problems until it jumped off a chair, was taken to a veterinarian, and X-rays revealed that the cat had a protrusion of a lumbar disc, resulting in a muscular atrophy of the left hind leg.

Animals may also become paraplegic and need immediate surgery. Cornell University's School of Veterinary Medicine is well known for its surgical treatment of animals for degenerative disc disease. Most dogs respond well and are able to walk again. Disc disease in animals may manifest itself by paralysis of the tail of the animal; the animal is unable to raise its tail when it defecates.

Animals may suffer from other malformations of the spine, which are also found in man. It is often pointed out that because of man's upright position he may have lordosis or scoliosis. In other words, it is suggested that these spinal curvatures are due to man's upright posture. This is another erroneous belief. Veterinarians can point out that other animals also have these curvatures of the spine. Animals, like men, also have congenital deformities of the spine. These congenital deformities may be life-threatening in both man and animal. If an animal so afflicted survives, it has an aching back, just as man would.

Evolution of the Horse

We have all been taught that the development of the horse is one of the prime examples of the evolution of an animal from a lower to a more complex form. Biology textbooks usually use the American Museum of Natural History's fossil horse series to demonstrate their point. This series includes the following:

1. *Eocene Horse Eohippus* is referred to as the "dawn horse" by the evolutionists. It is described as having been the size of a fox terrier. Each front foot had four complete toes, and each hind foot had three toes, the middle toe being somewhat larger than the side toes. This first horse had a short head and a short neck. The evolutionists believe that these animals roamed the Western plains of the United States about 50 million years ago. Remains were found in the lower Eocene formations of the Big Horn Valley in Wyoming. (See the artist's conception of the fossil foot bones of this horse, figure 2.1.)

2. *Oligocene Horse Mesohippus* is the name of the horse from the period of time approximately 40 million years ago. This horse was about the size of a domestic sheep. The head and neck are described as being slightly longer than those of the "dawn horse." The middle toes of the front feet had enlarged and the outer toes had shortened. All the toes of the hind feet still touched the ground; but the middle toe had become the largest. The body weight was primarily supported by the enlarged middle toes of the feet. This horse is found in all Oligocene formations of North America (fig. 2.1).

3. *Miocene Horse Merychippus* is the name of the horse

from the Miocene age, and is described as being about forty inches tall and about the size of a Shetland pony. The head and neck continued to become more elongated. The teeth are described as being longer and more adapted for grinding the grass which the animal fed upon. The middle toe of each foot had now become more enlarged and more distinct than the side toes, which had become smaller and did not reach the ground. This horse is found in North America in both the Miocene and lower Pliocene strata (fig. 2.1).

4. *Pliocene Horse Pliohippus* is a more modern-looking horse about the size of a donkey. The middle toe had

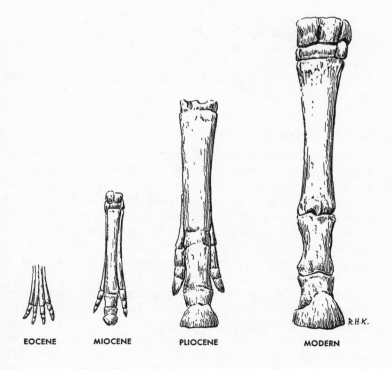

EOCENE   MIOCENE   PLIOCENE   MODERN

Fig. 2.1. *Courtesy of The American Museum of Natural History.*

enlarged more but had not yet developed into a hoof. The side toes were now without phalanges and had splintlike bones under the skin. This was the first appearance of the one-toed horse. The Pliohippus lived about 20 million years ago on the plains of North America. Its fossil remains have been found in the lower Pliocene formation of Sioux County, Nebraska (fig. 2.1).

5. *Pleistocene Horse Equus* came next. This horse looks like our modern horse. His head and neck were more elongated and he stood upon the middle toe of each foot. The nails had become hooves and the side toes were reduced to rudimentary bone splints. Fossil finds of this horse have been found in North and South America, Europe, Asia, and Africa. For some reason the horse became extinct in the Americas before the arrival of the white man. (The wild horses of the Western plains of the United States are the descendants of those animals which escaped from early explorers and settlers of the United States.)

Modern Horses with Birth Defects

The evolutionist either ignores or is stunned by any different interpretation of the "evidence" of evolution of the horse and other animals. But without doubt, these abnormal-looking fossil specimens are in fact congenital malformations (birth defects) of the animal rather than examples of an evolutionary process. This viewpoint is also true of the so-called "changes" in the skull of the horse. It is not at all unusual for multiple malformations to occur in an animal or in a man at birth.

For example, the so-called evolution of the horse's foot from walking on multiple toes to walking on the distal phalanx of the middle toe, can be demonstrated in present-day colts born with these abnormalities. Such a case of polydactylism was reported in the *Journal of the American Veterinary Association.* At birth an Arabian colt was found to have two completely formed digits on the left forelimb. These digits were surgically removed and an attempt was made to repair the skin cosmetically in order to produce a normal-appearing limb. Following the operation antibiotics were administered for five days. The wound showed satisfactory healing and the sutures were removed. When the colt was re-examined six months later, it presented a normal gait and a normal-appearing limb.

William Bateson, in *Materials for the study of Variation Discontinuity,* gives a description of a foal having extra side toes of the forelimbs. The young horse was the offspring of a normal-hoofed animal. Each digit had a small hoof, and the animal had difficulty walking with all three toes touching the ground. This resulted in injury to the tissues with inflammation of the foot, and the animal had to be destroyed.

Bateson states that the mare died two months after giving birth to its deformed foal. What was the cause of death of this mare? Was it an infection during the mare's pregnancy that caused her offspring to have birth defects of its forelimbs? Was this lingering infection the cause of the mare's death? We know that birth defects can be caused by infections in a pregnant animal or a pregnant woman. (See fig. 2.2 of modern horse with extra toes.)

In discussing the problem of malformations of the limbs of horses, veterinarians will readily admit that these abnormalities still do occur. A horse breeder usually wants an animal with congenital malformations destroyed so that, if there are any hereditary tendencies, the animal will not have a chance to reproduce colts with the congenital malformed hoofs of polydactylism.

Although sometimes only portions of fossil animals are found, they are used as concrete evidence of the evolution of the horse. We must not overlook the fact that there was probably more than one congenital malformation in a particular specimen. This is often true in animals as well as in man, such as in the mongoloid who has obvious physical defects as well as congenital heart defects and mental retardation. Therefore, it is a good possibility that the animals used as examples of evolution did not mature to the full size of a normal horse. It is also possible that they died before reaching full maturity because of other congenital defects.

There is also considerable doubt that the strata in which specimens were found indicate their geological age. Congenital malformations can be produced at any time. Harold G.

Fig. 2.2. Modern "horned horse from Texas," showing six extra digits. *Courtesy of The American Museum of Natural History.*

Coffin, in his book *Creation—Accident or Design?*, makes this statement:

> Although the specimens are reported to be taken from consecutive geological epochs, Eocene through Pleistocene, it is possible that errors had been made in the stratigraphy. Since the materials for some specimens are not abundant and since these fossils are seldom found in one area, there is room for the further study of the horse stratigraphy. The amount of time between the deposition of one stratum and the next is also in question. If some of these creatures were contemporaneous, the series as usually shown would be incorrect.

We have to conclude that what are called the fossil evidences of the horse's evolution are really examples of congenital malformations.

Dwarfism of horses is found today. Smith and Jones, in their book *Veterinary Pathology*, state that developmental anomalies ordinarily originate before birth. The frequency of prenatal malformations is surprising and their wide variety is unbelievable. These congenital malformations can be produced by the animal feeding upon certain types of plants or by virus infections.

Dwarfed or miniature horses are living today. For instance, there is a miniature horse farm near Gettysburg, Pennsylvania. The miniature horses raised there come from a horse breeder's farm in South America. The first mini-stallion, which sired or was related to most of the miniature horses living today, was only 20 inches high and weighed only 70 pounds (fig. 2.3). There are miniature types of all animals.

Human Tails

Human embryos are often compared to embryos of different species, and similarities in the early stages are often pointed out by evolutionists. They state that at the end of eight weeks the embryo becomes fully human. At this time it usually loses its tail and its fur, and its limbs then become hands and feet.

Here again the evolutionist makes some grave mistakes. He confuses a common Creator with a common origin. Because there is similarity in animals and man in growth and development from the fertilized egg into the adult, it does not mean that all came from a common ancestor. It does mean that the Creator used certain fundamental steps in the development of the embryos. (Often we recognize a great artist's paintings by his unique creative talent, which is his own style. Rembrandt had his own creative style. Likewise, the Creator had His own creative style, which is portrayed in the development of the embryos.)

Do human embryos ever have a tail? are babies sometimes born with tails? Do these human "tails" show a common ancestor with other primates? Compare the photographs of

Fig. 2.3. Miniature horse. *Courtesy of Gettysburg Miniature Horse Farm, Gettysburg, Pa.*

babies born with tails (figs. 2.4 and 2.5) with those of the primates, which have tails extending from the distal end of the coccyx (fig. 2.6). It is clear that the projections from the baby spines are in an entirely different location from the tail of the primate.

The opinion of two pathologists was that these fingerlike projections were more than likely fibro-fatty polyps. An embryologist was also very emphatic that this was some type of tumor or malformation, and felt that the location was definitely too high for any type of throwback, to show that we once had ancestors with tails.

By the early part of the fourth week, the neural groove fuses and becomes the neural canal (fig. 2.7). The cephalic portion of the folds eventually becomes the forebrain. The caudal portion of these neural folds is referred to as the "tail bud" or end bud. "Tail bud" is really a misnomer. In the human embryo there is never an actual tail extending from the coccyx, as is seen in certain primates, which in their embryo life and adult life do have recognizable tails. Compare the drawing of the distal caudal ends of the human embryos (fig. 2.8) and the monkey embryos (fig. 2.6). In the human there is no clear indication of a definite embryonic tail.

The reason that human tails are never described in medical books of pathology is because they do not exist. What is referred to as tails by some physicians are not true tails but congenital anomalies. In embryonic life, the area that undergoes the most profound growth changes is the nervous system. Because of these changes anomalies frequently result.

The fingerlike projections, which are found in many areas on the surface of the body, and very commonly in the lumbar and gluteal areas, are congenital lipomas.

The congenital dermal sinus is frequently found in the lumbosacral area. Its attachment may be directly under the opening of the skin or may go several centimeters deep and be attached to the spinal canal. Frequently these contain hemangiomas or lipomas.

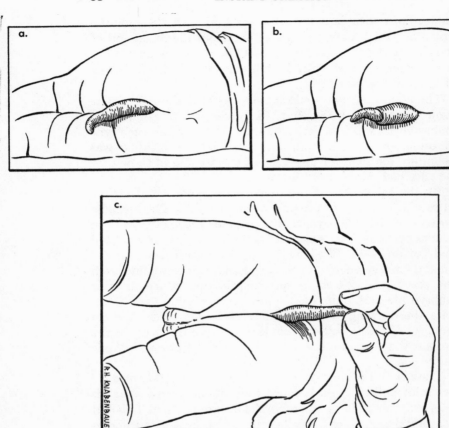

Fig. 2.4. Exact tracings of photographs from *Johns Hopkins Bulletin,*
April-May-June 1901. These photographs of an infant born with a
"tail" show the much lower location of this anomaly, which is the
failure of the neural groove to turn inward at this particular point. a.)
"Tail" from distal end of neural tube. b.) "Tail" showing contraction,
because muscle fibers in "tail" retract the skin (as muscle fibers
contract the skin around the anus). Real tails never have this
periscope-type of contraction. c.) Ventral surface of "tail."

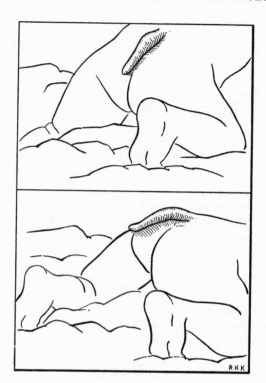

Fig. 2.5. Baby born with "tail" in sacral area. From Popenor, *The Child's Heredity. Courtesy Williams and Wilkins Publishers.*

Do such tails ever wag or move? It has been reported that they have "wagged," but this is questionable. If the muscle attachment underneath or if any muscle is extended into these fingerlike projections, movement could be possible. Lipomas attached to muscles may move when the muscles contract.

It is not unusual for animals that normally have real tails to also have an extra "tail," which is an anomaly.

The evolutionist proudly proclaims that this is a "throwback" to our ancient ancestors who once had tails.

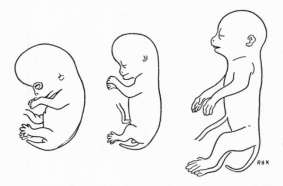

Fig. 2.6. Exact tracings of photos of Rhesus monkey fetus. From Adolph Schultz, "Fetal Growth and Development of the Rhesus Monkey." *Carnegie Contributions to Embryology* 26:71-97. *Courtesy of Carnegie Institute.*

This is evidence, they claim, that the human race has not completely genetically erased the tail from its inheritance. My research of medical literature finds that these "human tails" are pathological anomalies. Here again, the evolutionists have only a tale of a tail.

The Coccyx

Evolutionists teach that the coccyx is a vestigial remnant of our past ancestors. Recently, an evolutionist teacher of junior high school students told me that the coccyx is now a nubbin in comparison to the long tail of our ancestors. This teacher had accepted what was taught in the biology books by the evolutionists. He seemed to be quite upset that the coccyx could have any function in present-day, living human beings.

The coccyx is usually made up of four coccygeal vertebrae. Occasionally, there may be five and, on rare occasions, there may be three. The first coccygeal vertebra is much larger and broader than the other three.

The coccygeal vertebrae serve very important functions as

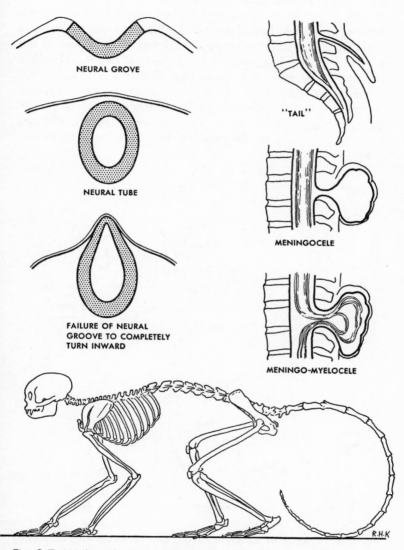

NEURAL GROVE

NEURAL TUBE

FAILURE OF NEURAL
GROOVE TO COMPLETELY
TURN INWARD

"TAIL"

MENINGOCELE

MENINGO-MYELOCELE

R.H.K

Fig. 2.7. Monkey showing tail coming off end of last sacral vertebra.
(All vertebrae of a real tail are coccygeal vertebrae.)

attachments for muscles. Their posterior surfaces serve as attachments for the gluteus maximus and the sphincter and externus muscles. The gluteus maximus muscle is essential in defecation and in labor during childbirth. The sphincter ani externus muscle is needed to keep the anal canal and orifice closed. These are very important functions. The normal curve of the buttocks is due to the gluteus maximus muscles. A person who has paralysis of the gluteus maximus muscle has a sagging buttock on the affected side. A person who has suffered an injury to the muscles that close the rectum will

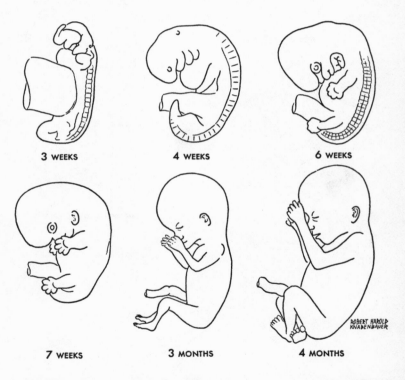

3 WEEKS   4 WEEKS   6 WEEKS

7 WEEKS   3 MONTHS   4 MONTHS

ROBERT HAROLD
KNADENBAUER

Fig. 2.8. Drawings of human embryos and fetuses showing no tails as seen in Rhesus monkey. *Courtesy Loma Linda University Anatomy Dept.*

have to use a device to protect him from sudden expulsion of feces from the rectum.

The anterior surfaces of the coccygeal vertebrae also serve as important attachments for muscles that aid in the containment of the feces within the rectum, in defecation, and in expulsion of the fetus during labor (fig. 2.9).

For these important reasons, the coccyx can never be classified as a rudimentary or vestigial remnant of our ancestors.

Other Vestiges from Our Ancestors

The so-called tail is just one of several ancestral vestiges that we of the human race still maintain as a part of our inheritance from our ancestors.

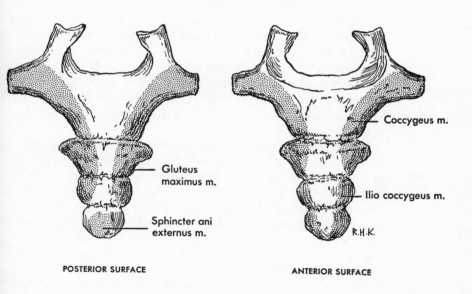

POSTERIOR SURFACE

ANTERIOR SURFACE

Fig. 2.9. The coccygeal vertebrae showing muscle attachments.

What is a vestige? By definition a vestige is a rudimentary or degenerative part, which was either functional in the embryo or in our evolutionary ancestors. These vestigial organs, according to the evolutionists, are dwarfed and generally useless after birth.

Let's examine some of these so-called vestiges.

Hair

In the fetal life of the human embryo, hair follicles and sebaceous glands begin to appear during the third and fourth months. Generally, it is not until the latter part of the sixth or the early part of the seventh month that these hairs of the human embryo are visible upon its body surface. These silklike hairs are referred to as lanugo.

Normally lanugo hairs are shed before birth or shortly thereafter. The evolutionists have made a big point of lanugo hair being a relic from our ancient hairy ancestors, and completely ignore an equally plausible explanation. Lanugo hair may well be the Creator's method of preparing the fetus for its future needs in the development of sebaceous glands, and hair follicle needs at puberty. At puberty, hair buds (or hair roots) in certain areas of the body respond to the hormones; pubic hair appears, and a boy who is maturing into manhood grows a beard. Here again we see the wisdom of our Creator.

Hypertrichosis congenita is a rare syndrome that has been found in some families. Affected families have increased amounts of hair on the extremities and the body. This transmission of increased hair is of variable dominant penetrance, so that all of the siblings will have hypertrichosis but some will be more hairy than others. I know of one patient who referred to her family as a bunch of "hairy apes." Excessive hair also can be reproduced in some patients who are treated for hypoglycemia with diazoxide.

Localized hypertrichosis sometimes can be found over the spine and is often associated with a birth defect in that area. Localized hypertrichosis of the top of the ear is a male Y-linked inherited characteristic. Hairy ears only appear in adult males and are transmitted by them.

After one young man learned this in a genetics class he was very upset because of the hair on his ears. He rushed home to confront his father with the bad news. His father reassured his son by showing him that his own ears had hair on the top of them. The father shaved his ears each morning. Needless to say, the young man was quite relieved because this is a sex-linked Y-chromosome inherited trait.

Gill Slits

Because human beings and fish have the same Creator, we share some likenesses in development from the point of view of comparative anatomy. But evolutionists over-exaggerate when they state that we have simple gills in our embryonic life similar to those of baby fish. Some fishes only have one opening on each side, and larger fishes such as the sharks may have up to five branchial slits.

Does having cervical fistulas (sometimes seen in the newborn, anterior to the sternocleidomastoidius muscle) mean that we have fishy ancestors? This is an absurd assumption by the evolutionist. As the pharyngeal arches (or folds) grow into their designated structures, the clefts or slits between these folds may remain open. This does not mean that we once had gills. When such a slit remains open, it is a congenital defect and can be surgically removed (fig. 2.10). It is no different from any other slit or groove that may remain open due to embryonic underdevelopment. This is sometimes seen along the spinal groove where sinus fistula may be present.

The thyroglossal fistulas may sometimes be found near the midline of the neck. Does this mean that we had anterior gill slits? Why can't this opening be called a gill slit? Here is another example of a birth defect in which the thyroglossal duct has some cystic remnants. This thyroglossal cyst is often connected to the outside by a thyroglossal fistula.

These slits or fistulas may also appear on the back and

other areas of the body; they are not exclusive to the neck. The evolutionists have not only exaggerated the similarity in embryonic life between man and fish but they have distorted the truth.

Wisdom Teeth

Another vestigial organ that the evolutionist claims is of little use to us now, is the wisdom tooth. This is not only a

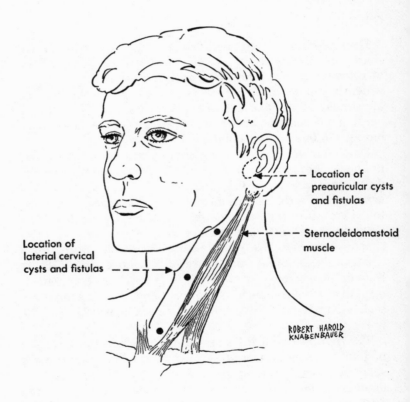

Fig. 2.10. Location of lateral cervical cysts and fistulas anterior to the sternocleidomastoid muscle.

fallacy; it is wholly untrue. It is generally held that diet and the amount of breast nursing a child has during infancy have a lot to do with the development of the jaws and teeth. Only some people have impacted wisdom teeth. There are many of us who have good, functioning wisdom teeth.

Extra Nipples

During the seventh week of the human embryo, the mammary ridge makes its first appearance. This is a bandlike thickening of the epidermis. In the human, the mammary ridge, which eventually becomes the breast in adult life, develops in a small portion of the thoracic region. Occasionally there is more than one nipple on each side (fig. 2.11). The evolutionists claim this shows our relationships to lower animal life, which may have six to ten pairs of nipples.

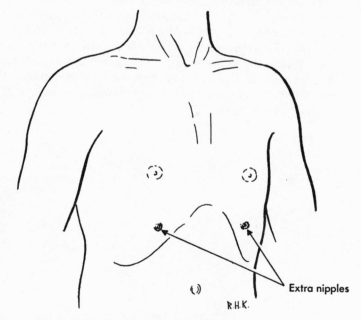

Fig. 2.11. Male patient having extra nipples.

Extra nipples show no more of a relationship to lower forms of life than do extra human toes or fingers. For example, one Arabic tribe is known to have six fingers on one or both hands.

I have never seen more than one extra pair of rudimentary nipples. Genetic mistakes can be made by the embryo: chromosome study frequently shows an increase in the number of X chromosomes in the cells of such individuals.

Appendix

The most famous vestigial organ of man is supposed to be the vermiform appendix. Just because we do not understand or know the function of the appendix does not mean that it is of no use.

Monkeys, apes, rodents, and rabbits also have a greatly restricted or almost semi-occluded lumen of the appendix the same as man. A thymectomy coupled with an appendectomy and performed on a rabbit leads to a very striking defect in the antibody response in comparison with a thymectomy alone. Since the human appendix has lymphoid tissue, it must be part of our immune defense mechanism, but it is most difficult to get research on the immune response of the appendix in a human.

3

The Origin of Man

From Molecules to Man

The evolutionist claims that chemicals got together by some electrical force and formed compounds which were able to duplicate themselves and eventually become a living cell. This is a great assumption which is mathematically impossible. This was so stated by Murray Eaton in his book *The Inadequacies of Neo-Darwin.*

Let us suppose that a self-duplicating molecule *was* formed in the oceans. This had to be deoxyribonucleic acid (DNA). In order for DNA to become effective and reduplicate itself, it must have the necessary amino acids, sugar, and phosphate available. If the original DNA was formed by some electrical or heat process, then a second discharge of electrical heat would destroy the original DNA. Since DNA is a protein and like all protein it is very sensitive to heat and pH changes, the electrical charge necessary for the formation of more amino acids (so that DNA can reproduce itself) would destroy the original DNA.

It is not within the range of possibility for DNA to be produced by chance. In Green and Goldberger's book *Molecular Insights into Living Processes,* they state on page 409, "... the macromolecule-to-cell transition is a jump of fantastic dimensions which lies beyond the range of testable hypothesis. In this area all is conjecture. The available facts do not provide a basis for postulating that cells arose on this planet."

The world's finest biochemists have never been able to make DNA from scratch. In 1967, DNA *in vitro* synthesis was accomplished by Goulian, Kornberg, and Sinsheimer. These scientists did not create DNA from scratch. Rather, the DNA was from a phage virus, which was unique in that it only had a single strand of DNA. When this particular virus with a single strand of DNA was allowed to enter into a coli cell, it was able to duplicate itself. This resulted in a double strand of DNA.

Does this mean that they created life? The DNA of the cells of your skin causes the cells to divide and grow daily. The food that you eat provides them with the amino acids, sugar, minerals, etc., that they need for normal growth. The *in vitro* synthesis of DNA only proves that this is the means by which these protein molecules can reproduce themselves.

The law of decay and death is also in action. D. E. Hull, in an article in *Nature* magazine, states, "The physical chemist, guided by the proved principles of chemical thermodynamics and kinetics, cannot offer any encouragement to the biochemist, who needs an oceanful of organic compounds to form even lifeless coacervates."

The following question always arises: If nonessential and essential amino acids can be produced in the laboratory, then why should the world be concerned about a protein shortage? Even if amino acids can be produced only in minute quantities, one would think that the large chemical and drug companies would want to produce the amino acids for the world's populations who are starving from protein shortage.

The second law of thermodynamics (all matter and energy tends toward a state of randomness or disorder) eliminates the possibility of the chance growth of elements into molecules, and molecules into macromolecules. It is obvious that there was a state of perfect creation which allowed the DNA to reduplicate itself by the available foodstuffs which were provided in the original creation. Certainly instant creation is more credible than the slow process of evolution. In fact,

DNA resists change or it would not be able to reduplicate itself. When a chemical change does take place, we have a disaster, such as sickle cell anemia.

Most evolutionists are not aware of a virus' nutritional and environmental needs. Under normal conditions a virus can duplicate itself only when the virus is within a bacterium, plant, or animal cell. A virus is dependent upon higher levels of life for its ability to reproduce itself.

It is easy for the evolutionist to claim that once a virus was formed it became a cell (such as a bacterium or amoeba). This is not possible, however, because viruses need living cells in order to multiply.

Thus, one can see that the evolutionists' claims are unreasonable.

Early Man

Is so-called "early man" really an early man? The skulls and partial skulls found by the archaeologists have been wrongly diagnosed by the evolutionists. The evolutionists believe that all primates, including man, had a common ancestor millions of years ago, and that all primates descended from this common ancestor. According to their thinking, the prehuman forms separated from this common ancestor into a distinct line twenty-five million years ago. The evolutionists claim that fossil skulls have the characteristics of both the ape family and the human family and that their teeth are manlike but their brain capacity only equals that of a gorilla or a chimpanzee. These prehuman forms supposedly have manlike bodies and upright posture. The evolutionists admit that the fossil record is very meager, incomplete, and that there are many "missing links."

Australopithecus

Some evolutionists believe that the Australopithecus is the oldest known prehuman. This ape man appeared about two to three million years ago and supposedly disappeared about a half-million years ago. The Australopithecus was found in 1924 by a worker in a South African quarry. The fossilized skull was examined by Professor Raymond Dart, of a South African medical school. Dr. Dart, an anatomist, gave it the name *Australopithecus africanus*. This means "Southern ape from Africa."

Java Man and Peking Man

In 1891, some skeletal remains were found on the island of Java, in a sand and gravel deposit. The portions of the skeleton that were discovered consisted of a skull, a piece of jaw, and an upper leg bone. Similar fossil remains have also been found in caves near Peking. The Java man is called Pithecanthropus; the Peking man is called Sinanthropus. Because these two men walked erect, the name *Homo erectus* was given to them.

Evolutionists believe that Homo erectus lived 500,000 years ago. One source estimates his brain capacity as being 750 to 1200 cubic centimeters. Another source states that this early man's brain size was about one-half the size of modern man's and only one-third larger than that of a present-day gorilla.

It is believed that Homo erectus reached the height of about five feet. He had a thick skull, bony, prominent supra-orbital ridges of the eyes, and a slanting, somewhat depressed forehead. He was capable of making tools, weapons, and fire. He was a cave dweller and probably a cannibal, since many of the skulls of the Peking man have fractures near their base.

Neanderthal Man

The evolutionists claim that Neanderthal man appeared about 100,000 years ago in Asia, Europe, and Africa. This early man became extinct about 30,000 to 40,000 years ago. Some believe that the extreme cold starved him out of Europe. But he also vanished from the Black Sea area, which is supposed to have been ice free. He was a short and powerful man who hunted large animals for food. Many fossils of Neanderthal man have been found in Europe, Asia, and Africa. His brain size is considered to be at least equal to, if not more than, that of modern man.

Cro-Magnon Man

Cro-Magnon man gets his name from the fossil first found in a cave in Cro-Magnon, France, and since found in various parts of Europe. This prehistoric race of people lived between 25 and 50 thousand years ago. Cro-Magnon men are considered to belong to the human race and are therefore Homo sapiens. They were hunters, and their tools were more advanced than those of the Neanderthal man.

Skeletons of Cro-Magnon males indicate that their height ranged between 5-1/2 and 6 feet or more. The female skeletons were proportionately shorter. The cranial capacity of males has been estimated to be 1580 cc. This is approximately 100 cc. larger than an average European male living today.

Besides being very intelligent, Cro-Magnon man was also talented artistically. He left beautiful pictures of animals painted on the cave walls in France.

Modern Man

The size and shape of skulls is no criterion of humanity. Since normal skulls of present-day living human beings may vary, it is doubtful that Neanderthal man was any less human than Cro-Magnon and Modern man.

The skull that houses the brain undergoes growth changes as it grows from infancy into adulthood. Under normal circumstances the skull is much larger at birth in proportion to the remainder of the skeleton. A newborn infant's skull is two-thirds the size of an adult's (see fig. 3.1).

By a marvelous mechanism the brain grows and the skull expands at the same time. The bones of the skull of a newborn infant are separated by serrated sutures (see fig. 3.2).

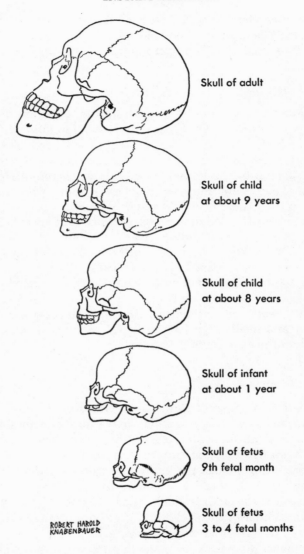

Skull of adult

Skull of child
at about 9 years

Skull of child
at about 8 years

Skull of infant
at about 1 year

Skull of fetus
9th fetal month

ROBERT HAROLD
KNABENBAUER

Skull of fetus
3 to 4 fetal months

Fig. 3.1. Drawings of skulls from 3-4 fetal months to adult skull, showing changes in size. *Courtesy of Loma Linda University Anatomy Dept.*

There are many abnormalities of the skull and many defects can be lethal. If the suture lines between the flat bones of a newborn infant's skull close prematurely, the result is a microcephalic skull or a macrocephalic skull.

There are sex and racial differences in skulls, which may not always be clearly distinguishable. The orbital ridges above the eyes are more prominent in the male than in the female. There is a muscular attachment on the skull that is also more prominent in the male skull than in the female. Because female skulls are usually lighter and smaller than the male, the capacity of the female skull is about 10 percent less than that of the male. Skull differences due to race are also recognizable. People of African descent usually have a thicker skull table than those of other races. There is also a variance in skull capacity. A normal, small-size skull (microcephalic) with a volume of less than 1350 cc. is found among the Aborigines of Australia. Those who are mesocephalic are the Africans and the Chinese, who have a skull capacity of 1350 to 1450 cc. The races which tend to have larger skulls are Caucasians and Japanese, whose skull volumes are usually greater than 1450 cc. The large skull is referred to as either megacephaly or a megacephalic skull. For more information see Isadore Meschan's *Rotogen Signs in Practice*.

Normal skulls may also vary in their shape (see fig. 3.3).

Microcephaly

Microcephaly is the term used when referring to small skulls. Adults who have a head circumference of less than 46 cm. (18 in.) are classified as microcephalic. All microcephalic skulls could have the same type of features that evolutionists point to in their fossil findings as evidence of man's evolvement from lower forms of prehuman life. In institutions for the mentally retarded we find many individuals who have microcephaly. Microcephalics often have heavy supraorbital ridges of the eyebrow area, and low, receding foreheads, as well as small skulls. It is quite evident that the fossil findings

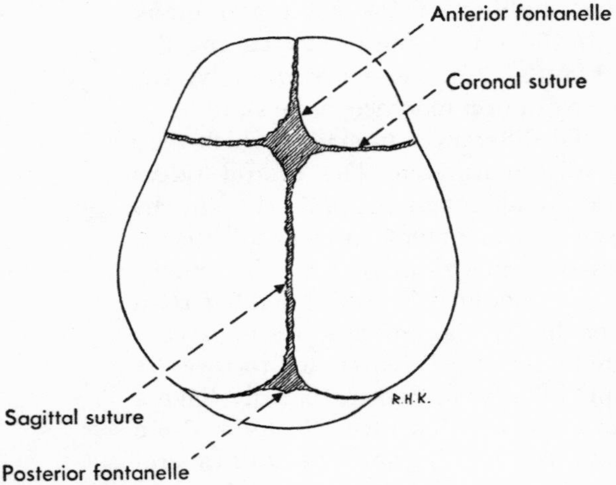

Anterior fontanelle

Coronal suture

Sagittal suture

Posterior fontanelle

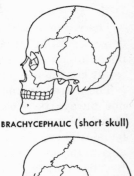

BRACHYCEPHALIC (short skull)

DOLICHOCEPHALIC (long skull)

Fig. 3.2. Skull of a newborn infant. Courtesy of Loma Linda University Anatomy Dept.

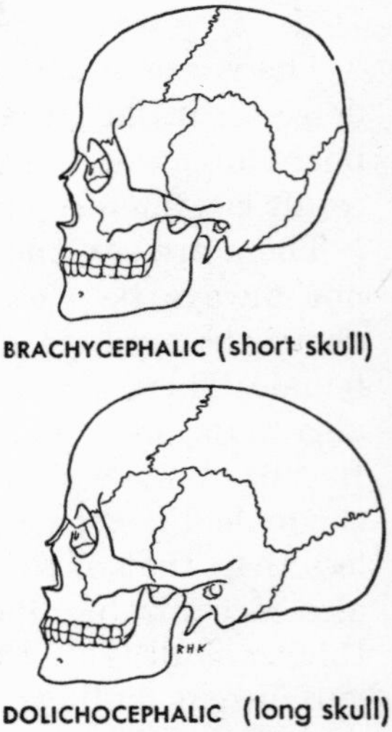

Fig. 3.3. Types of skulls. Courtesy of Loma Linda University Anatomy Dept.

Fig. 3.4. Microcephaly, familial. Courtesy of Dr. Sidney Gellis, Atlas of Mental Retardation Syndromes. U.S. Dept of Health, Education and Welfare, Social and Rehabilitation Dept.

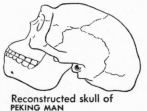

Reconstructed skull of PEKING MAN

MICROCEPHALIC skull of modern man, adult age

Fig. 3.5. Comparison of skulls. Notice that these skulls are very similar in size.

Fig. 3.6. Rendering of a baby, which I saw, born without a nose, with fused eyes (Cyclops) and a cleft palate.

of prehistoric early man are nothing more than congenital malformations.

The etiology of microcephaly is not always known. Because of the smallness of the skull, there is also a reduction of the brain size and mental retardation. Maternal infections during pregnancy may be the cause, or it can be transmitted by an autosomal recessive gene. Repeated cases of microcephaly have occurred in many families (see fig. 3.4).

Other Deformities

The evolutionists point to the similarity of facial features of early man and the ape as evidence of our common ancestral background. Many of these claims are based on an artist's conception of what the face of these fossil skulls looked like. The upper and lower jaws give the face these apelike distortions. The jaws can be small as in micrognathia or prominent as in prognathia (fig. 3.5). A depressed nose (saddle nose) or the absence of a nose entirely will also give fossil skulls an apelike appearance (fig. 3.6).

When a teacher presents these skulls as evidence of man's evolvement from lower forms of life, a student has the right to ask, "How do you know that these are not congenital malformations?" All students who are studying early man should visit the pathology department of a medical school in order to see skull deformities. They should also visit mental institutions, where they may view the deformed heads of living present-day human beings with skull deformities.

The Missing Links

Children first hear of missing links in elementary school, where they are taught that there are gaps in our understanding of the evolution of higher forms of life from lower forms of life. These gaps represent the absence of certain transitional stages in the fossil records.

Darwin, in *The Origin of the Species by Means of Natural Selection,* made a prediction concerning the fossil record:

> With respect to the absence of fossil remains, serving to connect man with his ape-like progenitors, no one will lay much stress on this fact who reads Sir C. Lyell's discussion, where he shows that in all the vertebrate classes the discovery of fossil remains has been a very slow and fortuitous process. Nor should it be forgotten that those regions which are the most likely to afford remains connecting man with some extinct ape-like creature, have not as yet been searched by the geologists.

As you can see, Darwin was convinced that the fossil record would confirm his theory of evolution. If evolution were true, the fossil record would produce these missing links. More than 100 years have elapsed since Darwin wrote *The Origin of the Species,* and the missing links are still missing.

When an evolutionist is confronted with the problem of the missing links, he may offer this typical answer: "The geological record is imperfect and will always remain so, since it is highly improbable that short-lived intermediate species will be fossilized."

One of the world's foremost evolutionists, Dr. George Gaylord Simpson, makes this comment about the absence of transitional stages: "On still higher levels, those of what is here called 'mega-evolution,' the inferences might still apply, but caution is enjoined, because here essentially continuous transitional sequences are not merely rare, but are virtually absent."

The evolutionary scheme shows an ever-increasing order of complexity; atoms become simple molecules, which then become macromolecules. Then comes the giant step upward of macromolecule to cell. For this step and for such a process to come about, great imagination is required. David E. Green and Robert F. Goldberger are biochemists who believe that the step from macromolecule to a cell transition outweighs all other evolutionary steps in enormity and is of fantastic dimensions. They go on to state that it is beyond any range of testable hypothesis; and that this transitional jump is all conjecture since none of the available facts provide a basis for postulating that cells arose on this planet. This can also be considered a missing link, since it is impossible for man, with all his technology, to make a cell. The finest biochemists are unable to produce a cell from a macromolecule. Is it reasonable to think that a cell was produced by chance as the evolutionists claim?

Instant creation is more logical and is substantiated by the sudden appearance of very complex and varied forms of life in the lower Cambrian strata. To the evolutionist this finding is an enigma, but to the anti-evolutionist it has been expected. Whitcomb and Morris give an elaborate discussion of the fossil record and the sudden appearance of fossils in earth layers in their book *The Genesis Flood.*

4

The Creator's Design
and Technology (Physiology)

The Cell

The cell is the basic unit of both animal and plant structure. It has been estimated that there are approximately one hundred trillion cells in the average human body. Normally each cell functions in cooperation with other cells of the body. This cooperation may take place by means of the nervous system or by some chemical process such as the hormone system.

A cell possesses some very interesting features. The cell membrane is a very unique structure. It is not a solid wall, but rather a membrane composed primarily of proteins and lipids. It is somewhat elastic and also contains pores. These tiny pores are the openings through which molecules of water and urea pass going into or out of the cell. These tiny pores regulate the flow of sodium and potassium, which are particularly important in the functioning of nerve cells. (See fig. 4.1, diagram of cell.)

As indicated in the diagram, the cytoplasm contains ribosomes. These ribosomes are the "workbench" of protein synthesis. The control of protein synthesis is under the direction of the "information center" of the nucleus. The nucleus of the cell has its own membrane, which is more resistant and tougher than the cell membrane. The nucleus functions primarily in the growth and reproduction of a cell. Within the nucleus chromatin material is found in the rest stage of the cell. During cell division this material rearranges itself to form chromosomes. Chromosomes are primarily composed of deoxyribonucleic acid (DNA). The DNA of the nucleus contains the specific genetic information for protein synthesis. This information is transferred from the DNA of the nucleus by a messenger RNA (ribonucleic acid). The messenger RNA then goes into the cytoplasm and attaches to the ribosomes. It is by this means that protein synthesis is activated.

Insulin is a well-known protein made by the beta cells of

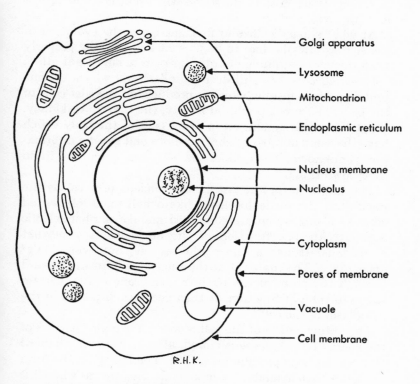

Fig. 4.1. Diagram of a cell's structure.

the islets of Langerhans in the pancreas. Insulin is stored in the beta cells and released when the blood sugar rises. This amazing, complicated process takes place without any conscious control of the individual.

Insulin is needed for the transport of glucose through the cell membrane except where the brain cell, intestinal mucosa, and tubular epithelium of the kidney are concerned. (See fig. 4.2, the chart of the structure of beef insulin.) After observing the complex structure of beef insulin, it becomes difficult to imagine such a process evolving.

When the islet cells of the pancreas become completely nonfunctioning, the patient must then take insulin by injection. If he fails to do so he will eventually go into a diabetic coma and die.

At what stage did insulin first appear in the evolution of the species? Insulin had to be present and working properly from the very beginning in order for man to survive at all.

Research chemists still do not understand why a specific protein such as insulin, which is produced in the islet cells of the pancreas, is not produced in, say, the thyroid or kidney. What turns this system off in other cells of the body which have the same number of chromosomes and genetic information is unknown. The cells of the body are specialized to do their "own thing."

The largest structure within the nucleus of a cell is the nucleolus. The nucleolus looks like a ball made of twisted cordlike fibers, which are composed mainly of ribonucleolic acid (RNA). The function of the nucleolus is somewhat mysterious. It has a "now you see me, now you don't" appearance. The material of the nucleolus diffuses outward through the pores of the nuclear membrane during certain stages of cellular function. It then becomes dispersed in the cytoplasm of the cell.

The mitochondria of the cell is where the major portion of the energy from glucose is stored, after it has been changed into adenosine triphosphates (ATP). The energy in the form of ATP is then available for immediate use, such as when it is needed for sudden exercise.

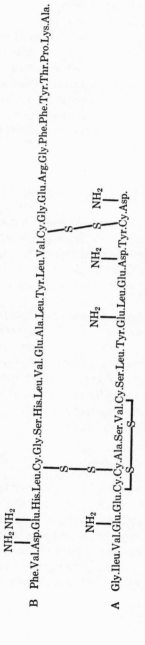

Fig. 4.2. Beef insulin is composed of 51 amino acids arranged into a unique structure for this pancreatic hormone. *From F. Sanger, Science 129:1340, 1959.*

The process by which glucose is changed into ATP is a complex system, and it is obvious that such a system took forethought and planning. We can draw an analogy here. The energy to make your car run comes from gasoline, which first came from the oil well and then went to the refinery, to the gas station, and then into your gas tank. Without question this takes planning and forethought. The process by which the cell makes energy is much more complex. A mind superior to a human mind was necessary to make this system function properly.

Automation

Automation, by definition, is the capacity for machinelike motion. In fact, the automobile gets its name from this word. "Auto" meaning self, "mobile" meaning able to move. The automation that we will discuss in this chapter is not the ability of man to walk or run, but the automation of the many functions of the body.

These automatic functions of the body's organs and tissues are controlled by the autonomic nervous system. This system of the body works automatically without our giving any thought to the control of it. Recently, there has been research done on self-control of blood pressure, heart rate, and bowel movements. There is some evidence that we may control our autonomic nervous system to some degree.

Let us examine some of the body's autonomic functions.

Respiration

Respiration is controlled by the respiratory center of the brain stem, which is located in the medulla. It is a complex system that sends out impulses causing us to breathe in and breathe out. The rhythmic cycle of inspiration and expiration is under control of the inspiratory and expiratory neurons of the respiratory center. There is interplay between these neurons, which causes the inhaling and exhaling to occur.

Inspiration takes place as follows: The muscles of inspiration are primarily the diaphragm and the external intercostals, which contract, causing inspiration. The intrapleural pressure and the intra-alveolar pressure change to allow inspiration to take place. Air fills the lungs as they expand during inspiration. As the lungs expand, nerve endings located in the lungs send impulses by way of the vagus nerve to the medulla, where they inhibit inspiration and stimulate expiration.

In expiration the muscles of inspiration relax and the muscles of expiration contract. The muscles of expiration are primarily the abdominals. An important factor in expiration is the recoil of the lung due to its elasticity. It is a complex system by which air is taken into the lung and then forced out. After expiration has been completed, the inspiratory center sends out impulses to contract the muscles of inspiration again. Thus, you can see how the cycle is repeated over and over again. This is the Hering-Breuer reflex. (See fig. 4.3, the diagram of the Hering-Breuer reflex.)

The rate of respiration can vary considerably. Under sedentary conditions, the respiratory rate may be between twelve and sixteen times per minute. During strenuous exercise, the respiratory rate may increase from two to three times the sedentary rate.

What causes the increase in the rate of respiration during exercise is not yet fully understood. It is believed that the motor cortex, while stimulating the muscles to contract by some means, transmits impulses to the reticular substance of the brain, which causes an increase in respiration. Increases in body temperature and in body movements are believed to be important factors in the increased stimulation of respiration during exercise.

When there is an increase in the hydrogen ion in the blood because of increased metabolism due to exercise or to diabetic acidosis, the respiratory center in the medulla is stimulated, causing the individual to breathe more rapidly. Chemoreceptors are located in the small aortic and carotid bodies of these vessels. These chemoreceptors have an abundant arterial

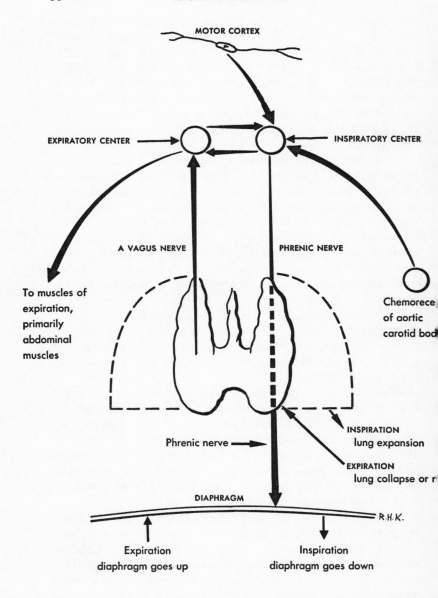

Fig. 4.3. Diagram of respiratory system and the Hering-Breuer Reflex.

blood supply. They contain neuronlike cells which are very sensitive to lack of oxygen in the blood, as well as to an increase in either the hydrogen ion or carbon dioxide of the blood. These nerve cells send their information by way of impulses along the vagus and glossopharyngeal nerves to the medulla. The information is then sent by way of the respiratory center of the medulla to increase the respiratory rate.

Can you imagine such a complicated system just evolving? This sophisticated respiratory system that causes us to inhale and exhale in a system in which one action brings about a counteraction. How did the evolution of inspiration survive when a counteraction of expiration also had to evolve at the same time? Here, again, we can see that there are multiple factors involved in respiration. The chemoreceptors are another example of an emergency backup system. A backup system is preplanned. We cannot wait for it to evolve. All systems' chemoreceptors must be ready to go when needed, as in exercise. The entire electrical system in an average American home is far less complex than the amazing system of respiration.

We still do not understand what initiates respiration at birth. Research has shown that there are limited respiratory movements of the fetus before birth. It is believed that the compression of the thorax of the baby when it is born may be a factor in starting deeper respirations when birth is completed.

We can control our respiration and breathe either quickly or slowly at will. Children often play a game of holding their breath. But it is impossible for a child to hold his breath for more than about a minute; he is forced to take a breath of air against his will. Sometimes a child may even become cyanotic (turn blue), but the respiratory system always wins out and the child will start breathing. This forced respiration by the respiratory system comes about when information that the child is lacking oxygen and there is a build-up of CO_2 is sent by way of the chemoreceptors to the respiratory center. The chemoreceptors are very sensititve to a decrease in the oxygen of the blood.

Isn't it a wonderful thing that the Creator did not give us complete control of our respiratory system? If we had the ability not to breath at all, there would be many dead children. The limited ability to control breathing enables singers to develop breathing techniques for singing. Breath control is essential for normal speaking and very important for public speaking.

Kidney Function

Normal kidney function is automatic. Under normal circumstances, we give little or no thought to our kidney function. The purification of the blood by the kidney was designed by a Super Sanitary Engineer.

Clearing the blood of impurities is not the only function of the kidneys. They help to maintain the electrolyte balance of the blood. The kidney function is an important backup system in maintaining the blood's normal pH. (This is more fully discussed in the section dealing with the backup systems of the body.) The enzyme systems of the kidneys know when to excrete the electrolytes or when to preserve them. Biochemists still do not know how the kidney knows to make ammonia from amino acids when there is an excess of hydrogen ion, as in acidosis.

The kidneys have a highly sophisticated ability to be selective. Under normal circumstances, they do not excrete glucose and amino acids. They also can concentrate the urine when there is a lack of body fluid.

This ability of the kidney to preserve water is very obvious. When someone is exposed to the desert heat for several hours, very little urine is produced. Such urine is more concentrated, having a higher specific gravity. The water that normally would have been excreted by the kidney is now used by the sweat glands for cooling the body.

The osmotic pressure regulation of the blood plasma (its viscosity as related to specific gravity) is influenced by the hypothalamus and the posterior pituitary gland. When sweating occurs, the osmotic pressure of the blood plasma is increased. The hypothalamus is evidently sensitive to an increase in osmotic pressure and sends this information by way of nerve connections to the posterior pituitary gland. The posterior pituitary gland responds to the information by releasing an antidiuretic hormone into the blood stream. This hormone then influences the kidney to preserve water for the body.

When there is a lesion of the posterior pituitary gland, there is a lack of the antidiuretic hormone. The patient then has an insatiable thirst. He drinks large amounts of water, because he is excreting so much of it in the urine. Thirst is believed to be due not only to the dryness of the mouth, but also to the increase in the osmotic pressure of the plasma. The process by which thirst takes place is not completely understood.

A patient who has the symptoms of excessive thirst and urinary excretion may have diabetes insipidus. Relief from these symptoms can be obtained by the pressor function of the posterior pituitary gland intramuscularly, which lasts 48 to 96 hours.

How could such a complicated system come into existence? All these many influences upon kidney function had to exist at the same time in order to function properly. There is beautiful cooperation in the automatic function of the kidneys for the needs of the body.

The kidney also has the ability to communicate with the vascular system of the body. When the blood flow to the kidneys is reduced, a vasoconstrictor substance is released by the kidneys into the circulation, which results in an increase in blood pressure. The complete role of this pressure substance on the body is still not clearly understood. It is believed to have some influence on the sodium balance of the blood and the control of the blood volume. It also raises the blood pressure by its reaction on the blood vessels to cause peripheral vasoconstriction and an increase in blood volume.

If the body organs cried out for the survival of the fittest, this marvelous cooperation would not be present.

Temperature Control

The body has a temperature-control center in the anterior portion of the hypothalamus. This heat-regulating center is divided into two sections: One is the heat-losing center, which reduces body heat when it is stimulated; the other is the heat-promoting section, which increases body heat when it is stimulated.

Multiple factors influence the heat-regulating center of the hypothalamus. When there is an increase in the blood's temperature, the heat-loss center sends impulses to the skin causing it to dilate and sweating to occur. If the environmental temperature reaches 115°F., as in the desert, the body uses this means to cool itself. (As mentioned previously, the kidney preserves water to be used in sweating by means of urine concentration.)

If a naked body is exposed to an environmental temperature below freezing, the body's skin will show vasoconstriction. A normal person, without clothing, when exposed to low temperatures for a long enough period of time, will eventually start to shiver. The heat-promoting portion of the temperature-regulating center then sends out impulses to the muscles to contract. Thus, muscular activity can increase heat production.

The Creator placed an automatic thermostat in the human body, which is superior and far more sophisticated than any that man has invented. It is yet another example of the body's emergency backup system. This particular backup system involves the cardiovascular system, kidney-function system, respiratory system, and metabolic system. The hormonal systems also have an influence upon body temperature, especially the thyroid hormone. When the body is exposed to cold weather for several weeks, the hypothalamus releases a hormone that influences the anterior pituitary gland to increase its production of the thyrotropic hormone, which, in turn, stimulates the thyroid gland to produce more thyroxin. By this means heat production is increased during the winter months.

What causes a fever? There are many causes, but the most common cause for fever is a bacterial or viral invasion of the body. It has been demonstrated that certain substances from these invaders of the body cause body temperature to increase and the thermostat of the heat-regulating center becomes "set" at a higher level. This higher temperature is lethal, especially to gonococcal and syphilitic invaders, and allows for increased chemical reactions necessary for the repairs of damaged cells. When a person is sick from an infection, it is essential to keep the fluid intake up so the body can also cool itself. Dehydration is an important factor when the temperature goes too high.

This well-coordinated backup system of temperature control had to come into existence all at the same time. Since extreme fluctuating climatic temperatures may exist from summer to winter, this system had to be working perfectly. While a hot climate causes one set of changes to occur, a cold climate will cause the opposite changes to occur. Such a system could not take millions of years to evolve because the need for regulation is not only from hot weather to cold weather, but moment by moment. One environmental effect would have inhibited the development of the opposite environmental effect. This elaborate backup system for emergencies of extreme changes in temperature required forethought and planning by a Creator in order to put it into existence.

Ponder this question for a moment: Could the thermostat control of temperature in your house have just *evolved* without planning and design?

Eye Function

Eye function is partially under automatic control but is also under voluntary control. The eye is a complex organ, which is, in simple terms, a small, living camera within the head. The eye is a masterpiece of design and expression. Not all eyes are perfect, but no man-made camera can duplicate what the human eye is capable of doing. Even the imperfect eye is very useful to us, and in spite of heredity flaws, the human eye far surpasses any visual instrument made by man. The fact that this living camera is so small makes it all the more wonderful. The eye actually focuses itself automatically and is capable of adjusting itself according to its distance from the object it is viewing and the amount of light coming into the eye. One's two eyes see slightly different pictures, but register them upon the brain as one image.

What is the mysterious power behind our vision? We all use our eyes for learning, and even a blind person depends on the vision of others for some of his needs.

The nerves of the eye are very important for the function of the eye. The optic nerve is the nerve of sight. It consists of fibers mainly derived from the cells of the retina. The optic nerve is a tract of fibers within the brain, rather than a cranial nerve. It is the connection of retinal nerve cells to the brain that gives us visual interpretation.

When the embryo is very small the optic stalks can be seen to have swellings on each end, which are the eyeballs.

Although we use our eyes for expression, the primary function of the eyes is for sight. To make sight possible, the light must enter the eye through the "window," which is the pupil. This window is covered by clear transparent tissue called the cornea. The cornea is a living sheet of cells many layers thick.

The eyeball is encased in a tough elastic coat. This can be demonstrated by placing a finger on the upper eyelid when it is partially open. If you gently press your finger back and forth you will see a distorted image, which moves in the opposite direction from your finger.

The elastic covering is the white part of the eye. On the inside, it is jet black. The black coating reabsorbs the light reflected from the retina. Without this black coating we would see distorted images. Beyond the cornea is the iris, which gives the color to your eyes. The iris contains muscles which regulate the amount of light that enters the eye through the dark aperture that is called the pupil. In bright light the pupil constricts by muscles in the iris, and when the light is dim the pupil dilates so that we can see more. This is automation. Directly behind the iris is the lens, which is surrounded by fluid and focuses the light upon the retina. (Each eyeball has a built-in thermostat to keep the temperature constant day and night.) This focusing of the eye is also automatic and a great optical feat. The shape of the eyeball itself is changed as we focus from a near object to a distant object or vice versa.

Each eye has its own window-cleaning mechanism—the lacrimal tears formed in the blinking of the eyes. Aren't you glad you don't have to remember to blink your eyes or to keep the cornea moist by the lacrimal tears? It is all automatic.

Reflex blinking is very important for the protection of the eye against foreign bodies. When something explodes near one's face the eyelids close and receive most of the foreign material. A child whose playmate throws mud in his face may have his eyelids and eyelashes full of dirt, but his corneas remain free of mud. Our eyesight also enables us to duck our heads when an object comes flying by unexpectedly—a most essential ability for a professional fighter.

The corneal reflex or blink reflex also aids the eye in the removal of a foreign body. When a foreign body is on, but not embedded in, the cornea of the eye, the eye closes involuntarily. There is an automatic increase of tears in the eye. This increased secretion of the lacrimal gland can cause a foreign object to be washed out of the eye. Many times a person comes into a hospital emergency room complaining of something in his eye, but before he can be helped, will exclaim, "Now that I'm here, I no longer feel anything in my eye." The foreign body will be found, most often, just below the lower eyelid.

Imagine what would have happened to the first eyes without this automatic reflex system. The eyes would have been destroyed by injury.

There are many other automatic functions of the body that space does not permit discussion of.

The Brain

The human brain is the greatest and most sophisticated "computer" that exists in this world. The brain can be compared to a computer, but is far superior to anything man can or ever will be able to make. What does this have to do with immediate or instant creation? Would an evolutionist be so naïve as to believe that sophisticated man-made computers evolved without design and planning? Computers are used to streamline savings banks operations, to keep track of parts and inventories in industries, to set printing type automatically, and to track space vehicles. Without the computer, man could never have landed on the moon. Computers didn't just evolve; it has taken years of research and brain power to put them together.

The brain has "components" similar to other computers in that both brain and computer have input, output, storage, and systems control. An athlete is a good example of the human brain's computerlike control system. (When we see a skilled baseball player giving a great performance, we always admire him and not the Creator who should be given his credit.) The ballplayer has superior eye, hand, and muscular coordination learned in his childhood, which enables him to play a very skillful game. When he goes to catch a ball in the outfield, he doesn't say, "Now I must look up, I must do this and run toward the ball" and so on. He does it automatically.

Memory and the storage of facts and information for our daily lives is seldom appreciated. How stored motor skill may save one's life is illustrated by this true story of a boy who learned to swim well as a youngster. Twenty years later, he was in a boating mishap that could have cost him his life had he not remembered exactly what to do in the swift current and just floated with it until he was picked up by a rescue boat.

It is not very often that the memory of a particular sound

will save one's life, but this happened during the bloody Congo civil war a few years back. When a certain missionary was a young lad living in the Congo, his black playmates taught him that the crack of two sticks in sharp succession meant a challenge of life or death to any intruder. They taught him the secret word to yell back, twice in succession, in answer to the challenge. During the war the missionary got into a bad ambush. He stopped the jeep and got into a ditch on the side of the road. When he heard the breaking of two sticks in rapid succession, he knew this challenge had to be met immediately by the correct secret word he had learned as a child, and yelled it back twice. This identified him as a friend of the tribe. The leader of the ambush called for the intruders to come forward and happily recognized the missionary as an old friend. The rebel leader was happy that he did not fire upon the intruders without giving them a chance to answer his challenge. This story shows how the brain stores information that may be vital to our survival.

Instinct

Instinct is a natural, inward impulse and behavior pattern, which apparently arises from the central nervous system of an animal or insect. Instinct rules behavior in life patterns of lower forms of life. The animal kingdom acts upon a locked-in behavior pattern called instinct.

Scientists have taken bird eggs of a whitethroat or garden warbler and hand-reared the young birds in a soundproof room. When the birds matured, they produced perfectly the characteristic and exceedingly elaborate songs of their own species, even though these birds had never learned them from their parents or other birds. We have to conclude that this pattern of singing must have been in some way coded genetically and stored in the central nervous system so that when the bird matured to the proper age, he could sing his merry songs without ever having been taught by mama or papa birds.

Do you think that this could have evolved slowly over

millions of years as evolutionists claim? Or was it put there by the Master Computer Programmer who created the bird? This Creator Programmer not only gave the birds a song to sing, but also built in other behavior patterns of the birds for mating, raising their young, and migrating.

Other interesting experiments that scientists have carried out on migratory birds involved rearing them in complete isolation indoors. The scientists wanted to find out by what means the birds were able to migrate from the far North to the South without the benefit of a compass. When the coolness of autumn began to be felt, and it was time for migration to the South to begin, the young birds were taken in covered cages to a planetarium. The birds recognized south, immediately took off, and tried to get out of the planetarium in a southwardly direction.

Long before man knew anything about computers, the Great Creator used computer programming in the central nervous system for the locked-in behavior of birds, animals, fish, and insects.

We know how to make and operate computers and how important it is for the computer programmer to put in the information that is necessary for feedback. There is a cliché among computer programmers, "Garbage in, garbage out." The information we receive from a computer relies entirely upon what information was put into it. In a like fashion, we can see the depth and wisdom of the Great Computer Programmer who created the birds and programmed their behavior.

The Backup Systems

The backup systems of the body, a well-planned fore-thought of our Creator, take over in case of emergencies. These backup systems could not have evolved slowly, because the very purpose of a backup system is to come into immediate action when the primary system has failed, or for some reason is not working in a normal manner and needs assistance from another system.

The buffer system of the blood is an excellent example of a backup system of the body. How could this buffer system have evolved? Here are the buffer systems of the blood:

(Plasma)	$\dfrac{Na^+HCO_3^-}{H_2CO_3}$	$\dfrac{Na_2^{++}HPO_4^=}{Na^+H_2PO_4^-}$	$\dfrac{Na^+ \text{ Protein}}{H \text{ Protein}}$	
(Red cells)	$\dfrac{K^+HCO_3^-}{H_2CO_3}$	$\dfrac{K^+Hb^-}{HHb}$	$\dfrac{K^+HbO_2^-}{HHbO_2}$	$\dfrac{K_2^{++}HPO_4^=}{K^+H_2PO_4^-}$

How could these chemical compounds be arranged so as to be a buffer to the blood and keep its pH within the normal range? Was it by the process of trial and error by evolution that these buffer systems became a part of the blood? Or, was it by a super biochemist Creator? The blood is maintained at a remarkably constant level of pH 7.3 to 7.5. Usually the pH is 7.35 to 7.45 in health. For the maintenance of this level, the body has four lines of defense: (1) the buffer system of the blood, tissue fluids, and cells, as well as the mineral salts of the bone; (2) the excretion or retention of CO_2 by the lungs; (3) the excretion of an acid or alkaline urine, and (4) the formation and excretion of ammonia or organic acids (see Kleiner and Orten).

The body has to maintain a stable internal environment in order to enable the various enzyme systems to operate under proper conditions and in relationship to each other.

The respiratory system helps to regulate the acid-base balance of the body. Carbon dioxide is the end product formed by all the cells of the body. Carbon dioxide combines with water to form carbonic acid. The CO_2 is expelled by the lung.

Where there is a high concentration of hydrogen ion in the blood, the respiratory center in the medulla of the brain is stimulated, causing the individual to breathe more rapidly in order to exhale and get rid of the excessive amount of CO_2.

Backup systems are too complex to just evolve. There is an automatic system which goes into action when the body needs to get rid of excessive acid in the form of hydrogen ion. The role of the kidney in acid-base balance is also very important. The body produces other acids as well as carbonic acid. These other acids include lactic acid and pyruvic acid as well as other important inorganic acids, all of which the kidney has to eliminate. These acids can be eliminated by being buffered by sodium.

In the case of a crisis, when sodium needs to be maintained in order to keep the blood buffered within its constant pH, the kidneys will produce ammonia from amino acids. In order for the kidney to excrete the excessive amount of hydrogen ions of carbonic acid, lactic acid, and pyruvic acid, as well as other inorganic acids produced in the body, it uses the ammonia it has produced to neutralize these acids.

The kidney does an excellent job in preserving sodium for the buffer system of the blood. Also, the kidney is able to get rid of excess alkali due to the ingestion of antacids by people who suffer from heartburn and ulcers.

How does the kidney react when starvation takes place? The body fat is used for energy. One of the by-products of fat metabolism is the production of acetoacetic acid. When the pH of the blood becomes too acidified, the kidney tubules enzyme system will change the amino acid glutamine so that NH_3 is formed. The acetoacetic acid is excreted as ammonium acetate.

We can draw an analogy here. When Apollo 13 went on its near-fatal trip to the moon, we heard a lot over national television of the backup systems being used to return the astronauts safely to earth. These plans did not come about by accident. They were carefully planned by the National Aeronautics and Space Administration (NASA) in case of difficulty out in space. When the command module's oxygen tank exploded, causing the command module to be nonfunctioning in certain areas, the astronauts used what television newscasters termed "their faithful LEM." The LEM (lunar excursion module) was to be used as the descent vehicle to the moon. Now it was to be used to get the astronauts safely home. They used the fuel of the LEM for their burns to get around the moon and put them in the correct projection to return to earth.

NASA clearly stated that all astronauts are trained to use backup systems in case of an emergency. This is carefully worked into the design of these magnificent machines that take men to the moon.

The delicate enzymes in the kidney tubules are heat liable. Our finest chemists cannot make them. This backup system had to be available when the emergency of too much acid first arose, and all these systems had to coexist at the same time. Each system's function is related to the other system's level of performance.

After studying some of the body's backup systems from a scientific basis, we have to conclude that the backup systems of the body are preplanned by our Creator for emergency use. It is certainly evident that according to evolutionist theories a patient in acidosis would die. The organism would never have a chance to develop a backup system and transfer it to its offspring since it would already be dead before it could reproduce itself.

Enzymes

Enzymes are specialized protein molecule catalysts that have the capacity to speed up the rate of a chemical reaction. There are over one thousand known enzymes, each of which is capable of accelerating a specific chemical reaction.

The enzymes work most effectively under definite pH and temperature ranges. The enzyme reacts with a substance which the biochemists refer to as a substrate. The end product of this reaction is called an enzyme-substrate complex.

Because an enzyme is so specific in its action on a substrate, it is called a lock-and-key fit. It fits like a glove. The site at which this takes place is called the active site or catalytic site.

This active site on the enzyme is comparatively small in

comparison to the rest of the enzyme molecule (see diagram, fig. 4.4).

How does the biochemist work with enzymes? When a suitable source of enzymes has been found, the tissue from which the enzyme is to be extracted is minced up with a sufficient amount of water. The extract from the tissue usually has to be buffered in order to keep the enzyme from undergoing irreversible changes.

Carbon monoxide inhibits enzymes containing iron or copper, as it has great affinity for the hemoprotein enzyme of the red blood cells. When enough of the red blood cells are tightly bound to the carbon monoxide, the oxygen cannot get to the cells of the body. Thus, the very sensitive central nervous system is deprived of oxygen and the cells of the brain die. If there is enough anoxia of all the cells of the body the patient will die.

What is hemoglobin? Hemoglobin is a complex protein that has the ability to combine with oxygen, forming oxyhemoglobin. The hemoglobin in the red blood cells then carries this oxygen to the tissues of the body. In the strictest sense of the definition of an enzyme, hemoglobin does not qualify. It is the vehicle by which oxygen is transported from the lungs to the tissues of the body. Oxygen has a strong affinity for hemoglobin and is tightly bound in the form of oxyhemoglobin while in the lungs, where the blood is relatively alkaline in comparison to the pH of the tissues, which is acid. When the red blood cell reaches its capillary destinations of the body tissues, it releases the oxygen because of the slight change in pH to a more acid pH. The

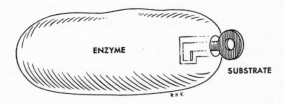

Fig. 4.4. Enzyme-substrate complex.

hemoglobin of the red blood cell in the capillary, after releasing its oxygen, is like a cargo ship. One of the end products of metabolism is carbon dioxide. The red blood cells' hemoglobin now forms, with the CO_2, carbaminohemoglobin. About one-fourth of the carbon dioxide formed in the tissues is returned by way of the hemoglobin of the red blood cells to the lungs. The remaining CO_2 produced by the tissues is returned to the lungs in the form of bicarbonate in the plasma. This amounts to about 60 percent of the CO_2 produced by the tissues. The remaining CO_2 produced by the tissues returns to the lungs as a physically dissolved CO_2 gas in the plasma. When the red blood cell reaches the lung again, it releases its CO_2 and takes on oxygen. The cycle is then repeated (see diagram).

The difference in gas pressures in the lung is another reason for the exchanges made by the hemoglobin of the red blood cell while it is in the lung.

Kleiner states that the globin part of the hemoglobin is responsible for the "specificity" of the hemoglobin of each species. This is such a complex system that the trial and error theory of evolution is impossible here. There is too much interrelationship between the respiratory system, metabolism, buffer system, and the red blood cells. All systems would have to be working and in perfect condition for a primate to live (see fig. 4.5., the diagram of oxygen and carbon dioxide transport by the red blood cell).

Enzymes are used in the metabolism of fats, proteins, and carbohydrates. In the complex metabolism of glucose to CO_2 and water, about twenty-nine different enzymes are needed. If too much carbohydrate is taken into the body, then the excessive amount of glucose must be stored as either glycogen or fat. Here again, different enzymes are used for the conversion of glucose into fat and glycogen.

Space does not permit a full discussion of the metabolism of proteins and fats. The body has a marvelous interconversion of major foodstuffs that are eaten.

It should be mentioned here that proteins are digested and then absorbed as amino acids, which are the building blocks

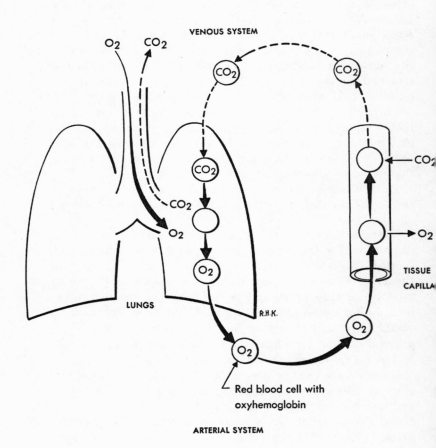

Fig. 4.5. Diagram of the red blood cell as it transports oxygen from the lungs to the tissues, and carbon dioxide from the tissues back to the lungs.

of the cells of our bodies. These amino acids are used in the protein structure of muscles, blood, and liver. In the human being, the end product of protein metabolism is urea, which is excreted in the urine by way of the kidney. It takes a unique enzyme system to perform this task.

Fatty acids that are taken into the body in the form of fats and oils can then be stored as fat in fat cells or metabolized in the body through the interconversion of major foodstuff in metabolism in the body.

Before leaving the enzyme systems, we should mention that enzymes often need what the chemists term "coenzymes." It is only when both an enzyme and coenzyme are present that the reaction will take place. Coenzymes are usually B vitamins and are a part of the enzymes' structure.

An element that is needed for enzyme activity is called a cofactor. One cofactor is magnesium, which is used in phosphorylation of glucose on its way to being metabolized.

As the reader considers the complex systems of enzyme activities he realizes that only by forethought and planning could such a marvelous system come about and be ready to act immediately. All stages of enzyme activity had to be present and ready to go. Only by instant creation could such a system come into existence.

In later chapters it will be shown that defects in the enzyme system can cause disaster or death.

The Cardiovascular System

The growth and development of the cardiovascular system of a human embryo is a fascinating subject. The vascular system first makes its appearance about the seventeenth day of embryonic life. The nutritional needs of the embryo require this development.

Three noticeable changes are taking place at this stage of embryonic development: Blood islands are formed; angiogenetic cell clusters are forming which eventually will become blood vessels; and the heart is formed from a single heart tube, which develops from a paired primordia (two tubes).

The growth and development of the cardiovascular system hold many secrets yet to be discovered. It is believed that hemodynamic factors influence in some way the formation of many small blood vessels in the early development of the cardiovascular system.

The Pump

The heart is a marvelous pump. No man-made pump can match it for size and capabilities. In a normal person who is at rest, the heart will pump approximately 5 liters of blood per minute. During strenuous exercise the heart may pump as much as 20 to 30 liters of blood per minute. During severe hemorrhage the amount of blood pumped by the heart can decrease to as low as 1.5 liters per minute.

The heart muscle is composed of interconnecting fibers in a latticelike arrangement. The two upper chambers of the heart are the right and the left atrium. The atria have thinner walls than the two ventricles.

The heart muscle has its own ingenious conduction system. It is composed of the S-A node, located in the right atrium, which is the pacemaker for the heart. Under normal conditions the heart rate is adjusted through the S-A node. Experimentally it has been found that epinephrine will increase the rate of discharge from the S-A node. The opposite effect, slowing of the heart, will take place when acetylcholine is applied to the site of the S-A node. It has also been found that stimulation of the sympathetic fibers of the cardiac plexus will cause an increase in the heart rate, whereas stimulation of the vagal nerve endings will cause a profound slowing of the heart rate. We know also that acetylcholine and the sympathetic transmitter substance have opposite effects.

How could such a clever system evolve? The evolutionists claim that environmental factors produce changes. Did the increase of heart rate evolve before the slowing of the heart rate effect? This would be impossible. We know that an increased heart rate over a prolonged period of time can cause death. Likewise, a very slow heart rate over a prolonged period of time can cause brain damage. It is only by instant creation that such an elaborate system could come into existence.

After the S-A node sends out an impulse, the atria contract. The blood from the atria is then forced into the ventricles. The A-V node, which delayed the impulse for a few hundredths of a second, permitting the atria to empty the blood into the ventricles, now allows the impulse to spread rapidly through the Purkinje system. This causes both ventricles to contract with full force, sending the blood out of the heart. Blood from the right ventricle goes to the lungs and the blood from the left ventricle goes through the aorta to other parts of the body. (See diagram, figs. 4.6, 4.7.)

The Monitors

The cardiovascular system has been provided with a well-integrated monitoring system. The Creator has provided a check and balance system, which permits necessary adjustments to be made by the cardiovascular system.

An increase in the blood's carbon dioxide has a very powerful effect on the vasomotor center. It causes an excitation of the sympathetic nerves to the heart, which causes an increased heart rate as well as an increase in arterial pressure.

There are many small nerve receptors in the walls of the arch of the aorta and the internal carotid arteries. They are very sensitive to any degree of stretch in the walls of these vessels. The information that there is an increase in the blood pressure causes an inhibition of the vasomotor center, which results in a decrease in the arterial blood pressure.

The regulation of blood volume is under the influence of kidney function, electrolyte balance, and the neural receptors in the left atrium, as well as the amount of antidiuretic hormone produced by the pituitary gland. It is obvious that

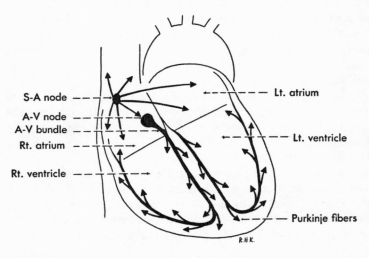

S-A node

A-V node
A-V bundle
Rt. atrium

Rt. ventricle

Lt. atrium

Lt. ventricle

Purkinje fibers

R.H.K.

Fig. 4.6. Diagram of the cardiac impulse's transmission from the S-A node into the upper chambers of the heart, then into the A-V node and then through the Purkinje System, causing the ventricles (lower chambers) to contract.

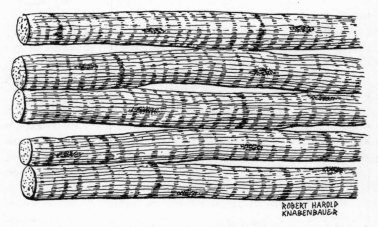

ROBERT HAROLD
KNABENBAUER

Fig. 4.7. Cardiac muscle fibers, showing interconnections with each other.

the various systems and body functions have a great influence on the cardiovascular system.

There are backup systems that influence the cardiovascular system only when there is an emergency. (See the discussion of the emergency of hemorrhage.) Without these backup systems survival would have been impossible. When an emergency arose, the cardiovascular system could not have waited millions of years for a plan to evolve to take care of it. The backup systems governing the cardiovascular system have been "designed in" by the Creator.

The Liver

The developing liver makes its appearance in the middle of the third week of the embryo's life. The outgrowth from the foregut rapidly develops into the liver, gall bladder, and a portion of the pancreas.

The liver continues to grow very rapidly. During the tenth week of development, the liver is about 10 percent of the total body weight. At this point in the liver's development it serves as a site for the production of red and white blood cells. The production of blood cells gradually decreases during the last two months of fetal life. At the time of birth, only a few small islands of blood production areas remain. In the newborn, the liver is 5 percent of the total body weight.

The liver has many functions besides the production of fatty acids, proteins, and glycogen. The liver has an effect on the regulation of the blood glucose level. After the digestion of a meal, the glucose enters the portal blood stream, which goes directly into the liver. Under the influence of insulin the glucose is absorbed into the liver cells. Within the liver cells the glucose is changed into glycogen. If the glucose blood level falls below the normal range, the liver changes the glycogen back into glucose. The liver will then release this glucose back into the general blood stream. The liver acts as a monitor for maintaining a normal blood glucose level. Glucose is essential for the normal functioning of the neurons of the brain. These brain cells will die if they are deprived of glucose. The liver has an important role in converting amino acids into glucose when there is a need for this production.

The Creator has provided a means whereby the blood glucose level can be maintained in periods of starvation. How could such a backup system evolve? When glucose is not available, most of the cells of the body can use fat for energy. The brain is the only exception. The liver is able to take fatty acids and convert them into glucose for use by the brain. This system had to be immediately available for the protection of the brain. It could not have waited millions of years to evolve. It had to have been available in periods of starvation when the glucose was not absorbed from meals.

The liver also produces prothrombin, which is essential for the coagulation of blood, and it is active in the production of urea from "worn-out" amino acids and excessive amino acids. The urea is then secreted by the kidney.

The liver is also a reservoir of blood. It has been estimated that the liver is able to release several hundred milliliters into the circulation if there is a need for blood due to hemorrhage.

The Kupffer cells of the liver are involved in the immune mechanisms of the body, as discussed under "The Unborn's Protection and Defense." The liver is also involved in the storage of minerals and vitamins. The liver has the ability to detoxify foreign substances that have been inhaled, absorbed, or ingested by complex chemical reactions.

A thoughtful Creator provided man with the ability to detoxify these foreign substances. It is a preplanned defense and protective mechanism, which only comes into action when there is a need. It follows then that this system of detoxification had to be instantly created as the poison would have killed before a system could have evolved.

The Gall Bladder

During the time that the liver is developing, the gall bladder and the cystic duct are also developing. The gall bladder serves as a storage tank for bile, which has been secreted by the liver.

The production of bile by the liver is a continuous process. The sphincter of Oddi blocks the flow of bile into the intestine. This forces the bile to go into the gall bladder, where it is concentrated to one-twelfth of its original volume. The gall bladder's mucosa reabsorb most of the fluid and electrolytes in the bile. The bile consists primarily of bile acids, cholesterol, and bilirubin.

In a 24-hour period, the liver secretes 600 ml. of bile. The gall bladder's capacity is only 50 ml. During one's three meals a day, the gall bladder empties. This means that the gall bladder has an amazing ability to concentrate the bile secreted by the liver.

There are two mechanisms by which the gall bladder will empty its contents into the small intestine. The first involves the hormone cholecystokinin, which is found in the intestinal mucosa. Fatty substances in the food cause this hormone to be released into the blood stream. When cholecystokinin reaches the gall bladder, the muscular wall of the gall bladder contracts, thus causing the bile to go into the intestine. The second method by which the gall bladder empties is by the relaxation of the sphincter of Oddi. As food passes into the duodenum, peristaltic waves are set up. The spincter of Oddi receives nerve signals that cause it to relax, and the stored bile enters into the intestine. The bile salts act as emulsifying agents on the fatty globules in the food so that there is a large surface area upon which the fat-digesting enzyme "lipase" can act. If a gallstone obstructs the flow of bile salts into the intestine, the fat in the food will be undigested. The feces will contain undigested fat and will be whitish in color because of the absence of bile salts. The bile salts give the normal brown and yellow colors to the feces.

There are essential fatty acids that are necessary in order to maintain health, and these fatty acids must be eaten. The body is unable to synthesize them, which means that the digestive system must have a mechanism by which the essential fatty acids can be absorbed from the food. It is only by a Creator that such a digestive mechanism could have been designed. It had to be instantly created, because of our need for essential fatty acids.

Infants who are put on a low fat diet may have a deficiency in the essential fatty acids. This deficiency of fatty acids can cause skin lesions. It was found that the addition of linoleic acid to the formula cured infants of their skin lesions.

The Skin

The skin is an organ that covers the body. It is as much an organ as the heart or the kidneys, and has vital functions to perform every moment of our lives.

The skin has some interesting characteristics. In the adult, it is about 10 percent of the total body weight. Since the skin has an elastic quality, it is under a slight amount of tension. This stretch effect gives a smooth appearance to most of the body surfaces. In areas of the joints there are lines and folds, which allow for the normal range of motion.

In the elderly, there is a loss of the elasticity of the skin, which results in facial wrinkles. If, by some means, the elasticity of the tissues of the face could be restored, there would be no need for any surgical intervention for a face-lift.

In the thirteenth week of an embryo's life, very fine lines, ridges, and furrows first make their appearance on the tips of the digits. There is a complex arrangement of these ridges and furrows that are acquired before birth. Each individual retains this pattern—known as fingerprints—throughout life. The only way that fingerprints can be changed is by altering or damaging the underlying dermis.

The deepest layer of the epidermis is the germination layer of the skin. The cells of this layer migrate upward as a sheet. As the cells approach the outer surface there is an increase in the amount of intercellular "cement." This cement causes the cells to stick together in a rather firm "togetherness" (see fig. 4.8).

Pigmentation

Most students are taught that the epidermis of mammals comes from the ectoderm. This is true, but the pigmentary system arises from the neural crest. The melanocytes are specialized cells that produce the melanin pigment. These melanocytes are found between the cells of the germination layer of the epidermis. The number of pigment-producing cells varies between races. Melanin granules are found in all layers of the epidermis of sunburned Caucasians and in dark-skinned races.

The amount of pigmentation of the hair of the scalp is under genetic control. The determination of the different shades and colors of the hair is determined by melanin and phenomelanin and the rate at which tyrosinase synthesis takes place.

Tyrosinase is the enzyme essential for the production of melanin. This enzyme is also know as "dopa." Albinos are unable to form melanin, probably due to the absence of the tyrosinase enzyme.

The presence of melanin in the skin of man serves as a light-protective system. It has been found that there is a

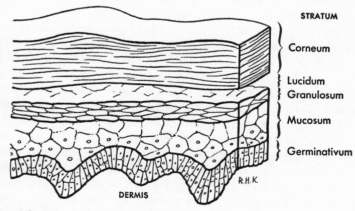

STRATUM

Corneum

Lucidum
Granulosum

Mucosum

Germinativum

DERMIS

Fig. 4.8. Diagram of the skin.

greater incidence of squamous cell carcinoma among the albinos of the San Blas Indians than among their relatives who have normal pigmentation of the skin. This has also been found to be true among albino Negroes in South Africa.

Light-induced cancers have also been found in Hereford cattle that have spotty pigmentation in the eyelids. These cancers appeared only in the areas where there was no pigmentation.

Investigators have discovered that melanin is a light-scattering mechanism serving as a protective shield from the damaging effects of ultraviolet light. Even with the protection of clothing we still need skin pigment. Albinos show the devastating effect that ultraviolet can have on skin that lacks pigmentation. It is evident that this process could not have taken millions of years to evolve. At whatever level coloring was needed, it was created instantly by the Creator.

Sweat Glands

The skin has two types of sweat glands, the eccrine and the apocrine.

The eccrine sweat glands are excretory. They begin to develop during the fourth fetal month, first making their appearance on the palms and the soles of the feet. In the axilla and other parts of the skin the developing glands begin to make their appearance during the fifth month of fetal life. There is no increase in the number of sweat glands after birth. As the body and skin grow, the number of sweat glands is decreased per square centimeter of body surface. In other words, there are fewer sweat glands in one square centimeter of skin in an adult than in the same area of a newborn infant.

The apocrine sweat glands are found in the axilla, the external auditory meatus, the eyelids, areas of the external genitalia, and the nipples of the breasts. These apocrine glands may differ somewhat from area to area in which they are found, but they are similar enough to share some general properties. The apocrine is secretory by function and is also associated with the hair follicle.

The proper functioning of the sweat glands of the body is essential for maintaining the normal body temperature. There is an interaction between the nervous system, the cardiovascular system, the kidneys, the body's temperature, and the environmental temperature. Proper functioning of the sweat glands is needed to maintain the body's proper temperature. When the environmental temperature is higher than the body's temperature the only way the body can lose heat is by sweating. By means of evaporation of sweat the body's surface temperature is kept lower than the temperature of the environment.

There are some people who are born without sweat glands and must always live in a cool climate. It would be fatal for them to be exposed to a desert heat of 115°F. Persons have died from an inability to sweat.

It is obvious that normal body temperature is maintained through the interaction of several of the body's systems. The absence of the ability to sweat can mean death. In order for such an elaborate system to function it must have come into existence instantly. It is quite apparent that the need for sweat glands could not have waited millions of years to evolve.

5

Motion

The Physiology of Motion

The study of the motion of the body, involving the nervous system, the muscular system, and the skeletal system, can be very intriguing.

Body motion involves the ability to ambulate—to walk or to move about. The ability of a person to walk seems to be an ordinary function of life, and is never fully appreciated until we see someone who is unable to ambulate. Patients who have had a temporary paralysis are most appreciative of the return of the capability of movement.

Normal Gait

The biomechanics of the normal human gait is a complex process. It permits the body to be moved by well-controlled and coordinated movements, which permit a smooth path for the body's center of gravity to move through as we walk.

It is easy to demonstrate this process. If you have normal lower extremities, walk for a few steps. Then walk with one shoe off. You will immediately notice that your gait is no longer smooth, but jerky and uncomfortable. There is an "unreal" discrepancy in the length of your lower extremities that makes walking very uncomfortable. If you had to walk this way all the time, you would soon have traumatic arthritis of the joints of your spine as well as the joints of your lower extremities. This frequently happens to people who refuse to wear a shoe lift on the shorter extremity when there is a difference in the length of their legs.

When a forward step takes place, it involves two phases:

1. *Stance Phase.* The stance phase is that period of time in which the foot or part of the foot is in contact with the floor. This includes the heel strike, mid-stance, and push-off. The stance phase begins when the heel strikes the floor and ends when the great toe pushes off the floor.

2. *Swing Phase.* This phase begins when the toe leaves the floor and ends when the forward motion of the leg ceases. As the leg begins its motion, it accelerates and then decelerates. This deceleration is brought about by the hamstring muscles on the posterior aspect of the thigh.

There is a short period of time in which both feet are in contact with the floor. This is the "double-support" phase.

What protects us from jolts as we walk? The knee joint, the ankle joint, and the heel act as shock absorbers.

The interaction of the muscles is essential for normal gait. By electromyography the interaction of these muscles has been demonstrated. For example, the quadriceps not only extends (straightens) the lower leg, but also prevents the heel from rising too high off the floor. In other words, this double action of the quadriceps prevents us from kicking ourselves in the buttocks with our heels as we walk. (See fig. 5.1.)

Normally the pelvis rotates about 4 degrees forward with each step. To demonstrate this, put your hands on your hips and walk normally. Now walk taking some giant steps. This demonstrates that the pelvis rotates forward as we walk.

During normal gait there is reciprocal action of the upper extremities. The diagram of normal gait best demonstrates this. (See fig. 5.1.)

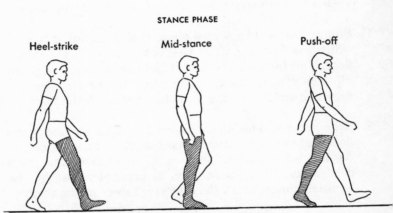

Foot in contact with floor, body weight on RIGHT leg

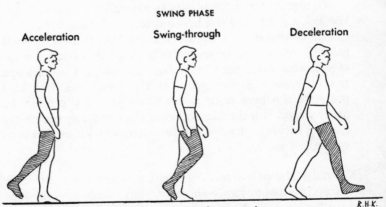

Foot not in contact with floor, body weight on LEFT leg

Fig. 5.1. Phases of walking. (*Courtesy Charles C. Thomas Publishers. From Clinical Prosthetics for Physicians and Therapists, M. H. Anderson, et al.*)

The best way to notice the difference between running and walking is to watch a track meet on television. Most of the participants are experts in track. In running, the heel portion of the foot strikes the ground first and the strides are further apart. As you look at a runner from the side, you will immediately notice that both his knees go higher off the ground than when walking. This allows for more length in each stride.

Nervous System Control

A former track star was a wide receiver for the Dallas Cowboys football team. His running ability and his good eye-hand coordination, which enabled him to catch the ball, have paid off financially. His excellent coordination is due to a highly sophisticated nervous system.

The cerebellum plays an important role in movement. For example, if you wish to pick up a pencil your hand can move to the position where the pencil is and pick it up.

The cerebellum aids in this movement by acting on the information it receives from the eyes and cerebral cortex. The cerebellum prevents overshoots. It receives information from the moving extremities of the body and then sends information back to the motor cortex that can slow up or stop the movement.

What happens when the cerebellum is not functioning? A patient who has cerebellar disease will have jerky and uneven movements in contrast to a normal person's smooth movements. A patient with marked cerebellar disease will have a difficult time controlling his balance, and will stagger from side to side.

The cerebellum is essential for walking. People who are under the influence of alcohol will often have a staggering gait due to the suppression of the action of the cerebellum by the alcohol.

Experiments have been done on monkeys where portions of the cerebellum are destroyed. These monkeys were unable to judge their speed while running, and would run into walls and bash their heads.

The interaction of the various systems of the body is necessary for body movement. At what level did these mechanisms evolve? These systems are interrelated and are essential for movement of the body. The cerebellum is a backup control system, which tells the motor cortex to go ahead, to stop, or to speed up. It is evident that it had a Designer.

Wherever well-coordinated movement is needed, all these systems had to be created instantly and intact. Otherwise the animal would not have been able to survive. How could environmental factors influence the evolution of the cerebellum? Its ability to collect information and tell the motor cortex whether to go ahead, stop, or go faster is a computerlike function.

The evolutionist believes that environmental factors influence the development of organs. If there was a need, then there would be an evolution of the particular organ that would satisfy this environmental need. In the case of the cerebellum, the need to stop a movement would be erased by the need to start a movement.

The highly complex influence of the cerebellum on body movement can only be explained by instant creation.

The Hand

The anatomy of the normal human hand is pure perfection. Its design cannot be improved upon.

At the beginning of the fifth week of the embryo's life, the limb buds appear. It is obvious that the upper limb buds will become the upper extremities and the lower limb buds will become the lower extremities. By the sixth week of the human embryo's life, the hand becomes recognizable. The development of the upper extremities is always more advanced than the development of the lower extremities. This is demonstrated in the photograph of a six-week-old human embryo in the chapter on human tails.

As the limb buds elongate, the muscular tissue begins to

differentiate into the flexor group of muscles and the extensor group of muscles. As the muscles develop, they bring along their nerve and blood supply. All this is accomplished in a very orderly fashion, showing that a Designer laid out a plan for the development of the extremities.

Several years ago the medical world was shaken by the increased number of abnormalities in newborn infants caused by the use of thalidomide in early pregnancy. Frequently these abnormalities involved the limbs. The mothers of affected children had taken thalidomide during their early pregnancies. In some ways the thalidomide had a devastating effect on these children when they were tiny embryos.

The function of the normal hand is very complex and is dependent not only upon the normal functioning of the joints of the hand and wrist but also of the elbow and shoulder. For example, a patient who has both shoulders "frozen" is unable to comb her hair satisfactorily. And a patient who has lost his ability to bend his right elbow will have to use his left hand in order to eat.

The inability of an individual to rotate the lower arm from an inward to an outward position can cause difficulty in the use of a spoon. The next time you eat a meal, try to use your fork without rotating your wrist and lower arm. You will immediately see that it is more difficult to eat if you do not have the rotation of your wrist and elbow.

The hand has a prehensile ability, which means the ability to grasp. The grasping patterns of the hand vary with the shape of the object that the hand takes hold of. The normally functioning hand can write with a pencil, pick up a needle, carry a suitcase, grasp a baseball, and perform many other grasping functions.

An individual who has lost a hand knows that an artificial hand or a hook cannot compare with the normal human hand. Only people who have lost both hands will rely on hooks.

Without skilled hands we would be without art. The hands can make buildings and machines, as well as beautiful paintings.

It is a highly complex skill to be able to play the piano. The talents of great musicians defy the theory of evolution. Music is not essential for survival, but it does make our lives more enjoyable.

The question arises, how could the talent for art evolve? What environmental force caused it to evolve? Man's artistic ability was given to him by the Creator.

The normal functioning of the hand is essential for our well-being. How could the opening and closing of the hand take millions of years to evolve? Only by instant creation could these functions of the hand come about.

In order to have a normally functioning hand the nervous system must have certain vital information: pain, touch, pressure, and position sense. This information allows the muscles that move the hand and fingers to adjust to the size, shape, texture, weight, and temperature of the object involved. This information goes to large areas of the cerebral cortex. The total cortical area for the remainder of the upper extremities, the body, and the lower extremities is only slightly larger than the total cortical area for the hands.

The nervous system controls the highly complex hand functions. This is obvious in persons who have no upper extremities. Some have learned to eat and write with their feet. But they are, obviously, not able to function as well as an individual with normally functioning hands.

Artificial hands and hooks have been designed by a human mind. The design of these artificial hands and hooks is much less complicated than the human hand. The human hand, as well as the artificial hand and hook, had a Creator.

Birds

When I was a youngster I heard of people who were birdwatchers. I wondered why anyone would want to watch birds. I noticed that birds were never still very long but were always on the go. I always wished that they would linger a little longer and be more friendly.

One day my older brother brought home two baby crows. He fed and cared for them for several weeks. The young crows were very playful and would swallow my brother's marbles, then regurgitate them. They knew the difference between corn and marbles, for they never regurgitated corn.

The crows were eventually returned to the wilds, and I often wondered how long they survived on their own.

The Evolution of Birds

What is the fossil record concerning the evolution of birds? We have been taught that birds evolved from reptiles. The fossil records show no transitional stages between the reptile and the bird.

The feathers of a bird are supposed to be modified reptilian scales. This is foolishness. In order for reptilian scales to change into feathers the DNA of the cells would have to have the pattern for feathers. The explanation that the jumping of reptiles from tree to tree caused this change is ridiculous. Why doesn't the bat have feathers? Why didn't the bat develop feathers like a bird in order to fly?

Some birds require flight in order to reach their feeding grounds. Can you imagine the ancestor of a small sparrow being able to survive before it developed the ability to fly? The requirement of feathers for flight was an immediate demand for the survival of certain birds. No explanation but instant creation is adequate for the existence of the mechanism of flight in certain birds.

Birds who do not fly, such as ostriches, are said to have vestigial wings. But what would happen to their balance if their wings were amputated? Their mobility would be severely impaired.

Migration

The migration of birds has always interested mankind. The ability of birds to navigate to an exact point thousands of miles away was a puzzle and baffled the minds of men.

In 1919 Baldwin demonstrated the remarkable precision of bird navigation. By putting a band on a bird's leg he demonstrated that white-throated sparrows flew south to Georgia to live during the winter months.

The ability of the birds to navigate remained obscure until 1946, when Ising postulated birds' navigation was accomplished by the "Coriolis force." The Coriolis force is the mechanical effect that results from the rotation of the earth. This force is zero at the Equator and is the strongest at the North and South Poles. There are other factors that influence the bird's ability to use the Coriolis force, such as the speed of the bird's flight and wind resistance. Wynne-Edwards showed in 1948 that a change of only one mile per hour in the bird's flight speed would alter the Coriolis force and the bird would land 150 miles away from the nesting area (see Van Tyne and Berger).

In 1949 a Polish investigator suggested an old theory that birds were migrating to a warmer area because of infrared rays. This theory does not explain the northward migration of the birds in the spring of the year, and is not acceptable as an explanation of bird navigation.

Other studies have shown that birds use the sun and the stars in their navigational feats. How could such a complex system evolve? Isn't it possible that Someone programmed the birds to use the celestial bodies for navigation?

Feeding

Birds have the ability to know when walnuts are ready to be picked from a tree. The bluejays never seem to bother my walnut tree until the outer husk that covers the walnut begins to crack open. All day long the bluejays pick walnuts from my tree and then bury them in the empty lot next door to my house—but never until the walnuts are ripe. It is a marvelous thing that the bluejays and other birds know when the walnuts are ripe. Otherwise, they would pick the unripe walnuts and destroy the crop. Who gave the bluejays the ability to know when the walnuts are ripe?

All of these marvelous abilities that the birds have were put there by the Creator. In order for birds to survive, they had to have all systems ready to go when they came into existence. Some birds could not survive if they did not have the ability to fly and to navigate to an exact point.

Those of us who drive sometimes get lost and lose our sense of direction. We have no built-in navigational system. If all the directional signs on the roads and the freeways were taken down, how long would it take for a human being to evolve an elaborate navigational system such as the birds have? Is this absurd? So is the theory of the evolution of birds. It is only by instant creation that birds have this marvelous navigational ability.

6

The Body's Protection and Defense Systems

The Hemorrhage Emergency

By what mechanism is death from hemorrhage prevented? Blood coagulation (a marvelous mechanism within the blood itself) prevents blood loss from vessels that have been severed.

Under normal circumstances, the platelets of the blood are negatively charged and they repel each other because of their negative charge. The platelets rupture when they are exposed to air or when they are injured. The platelets then release thromboplastin, which reacts upon the prothrombin in the blood to form thrombin. The thrombin then reacts with the fibrinogen in the blood and with calcium to form fibrin. A fibrin net is formed within and around the vessel, which serves to plug it up.

The steps in the prompt process of blood coagulation can be interfered with at several locations. We have known for a long time that vitamin K is used in the synthesis of prothrombin in the liver. Vitamin K is produced by bacterial activity in the lower intestinal tract, absorbed by the blood stream, and used by the liver to produce prothrombin. In ulcerative colitis it may be necessary to give vitamin K by injection in order for the patient to produce enough pro-thrombin. Vitamin K is particularly useful when a patient who has ulcerative colitis is going to undergo surgery.

Suppose that there is plenty of vitamin K produced by the bacterial flora in the intestine, but the patient has a diseased liver and is unable to produce prothrombin. If a patient has a problem of blood clotting within the vascular system, his physician can order coumadin, which can prevent prothrombin from being formed by the liver, thus lowering the ability of the blood to coagulate.

Blood banks use a very simple process to prevent coagulation of stored blood. The blood drawn from a donor goes into a plastic container that contains CPD (citrate phosphate dextrose). This combines with the calcium to form an insoluble compound called sodium oxalate or sodium citrate. Thus fibrinogen cannot form fibrin because the calcium, which is necessary for this process to take place, is tied up in an insoluble form as sodium oxalate. Such blood can be stored and later given to a patient.

Hemophilia is a hereditary disease caused by the lack of an essential factor in the clotting process. This factor not present in the hemophiliac blood is referred to as the antihemophiliac globulin. Hemophilia A has the enzyme factor 8 missing. Hemophilia B has the enzyme factor 9 missing. Parahemophilia has the enzyme factor 5 missing. As more research is being done on hemophilia, other enzymes may be found to be missing in the hemophiliac's blood when compared to normal blood.

A hemophiliac may need a standing order at his local community hospital for antihemophiliac globulin plasma whenever he has an episode of bleeding into the joints or from small trauma.

Queen Victoria was a famous progenitor of hemophiliacs. Hemophilia is an X-linked trait carried on the X chromosome. It is a recessive characteristic that acts in a dominant way when inherited by the male. This is because men have only one X chromosome from the mother and one Y chromosome from the father. Queen Victoria had two daughters who became carriers of hemophilia. Only one of her six sons, Leopold, the Duke of Albany, inherited the hemophiliac trait. Leopold died of the disease at the age of 31.

(See fig. 6.1 on the transmission of hemophilia by Queen Victoria to her descendants.)

Intravascular clots are prevented by several factors. The two most important are the negative charge on platelets and heparin, which is circulating in the blood.

Researchers have demonstrated that the endothelial lining of blood vessels has a negative charge on cell membranes. Since the platelets also have a negative charge on their cell membranes, they repel each other and therefore prevent clotting.

Heparin, which is produced by the liver, is found in a very small quantity in the blood stream. (See fig. 6.2, diagram on the process of the coagulation of blood, which shows the points at which heparin interferes with coagulation.)

How could this complicated process have evolved? The evolutionists claim that environment brings about change. When enzyme A brings about a certain reaction, another enzyme, B, inhibits enzyme A from reacting. This is clearly illustrated in the case of hemophilia. It is such a highly complex process that all enzymes must be present and functioning properly in order for the human being to live. Queen Victoria's son, Leopold, died because he lacked one of these antihemophiliac factors.

The Healing Process

In order for healing and repair to take place, many of the body's systems must be involved. Some of these systems are very complex and space will not permit a lengthy discussion.

How does a wound undergo regeneration and repair? The process of healing takes place in a very orderly manner, which involves the following processes.

Cellular Regeneration

When there is a superficial injury to the upper layers of the skin there is no bleeding. The deeper layer of the skin, under

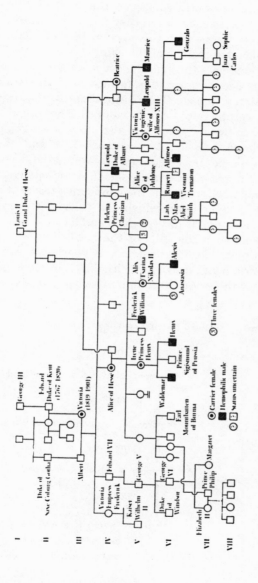

Fig. 6.1. Pedigree of Queen Victoria and her descendants, illustrating the transmission of hemophilia, an X-linked recessive trait. *From Victor A. McKusick, Human Genetics, 2nd edition.*

the cornium, is uninjured. Since the cells of the skin are firmly attached to each other, they migrate upward as a sheet of cells. Most frequently, this type of healing takes place in very superficial abrasions of the skin.

If the wound goes through the deepest layer of the skin and hemorrhage occurs, a crust is formed over the wound from the coagulated blood. The formation of the crust is a temporary protection of the wound. The crust forms a protection against infection and also stops the leaking of fluid from the injured tissue. As the crust dries and hardens, it serves as a temporary closure of the wound. Under the crust the healing process is taking place. The mesenchyme, which is embryonic in character, is the connective tissue of the body and forms a layer upon which the cells of the epithelium migrate. If a wound is not too deep and has not destroyed the mesenchyme, then the cells of the epithelium will begin to migrate at once, closing the defect. A layer of mesenchyme is always necessary in order for epithelial cellular migration to take place if the wounds are more than skin deep.

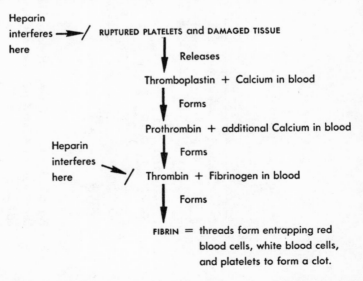

Fig. 6.2. Schematic drawing of the major steps in blood coagulation.

Some wounds are healed simply by the migration of the cells of the epithelium. This occurs in superficial wounds of the cornea of the eye when only the epithelial layer is involved. The epithelial cells of the cornea will move in and close a defect in six hours. Fast healing has also been observed in very small wounds of the skin where cell division plays no part in closure of the wound. This type of closure is accomplished entirely by cell migration.

In large wounds cell division becomes more frequent after an initial stage of inhibition of cell division. Cell replacement is normal in some of our organ systems. This occurs normally in the skin and also in the replacement of red blood cells by the bone marrow. When the "wear-and-tear" of cells is at a lower level, such as in the liver, the rate of replacement of these cells is very low until there is a need for repair of the organ and it is stimulated to replace the damaged cells.

There are some cells of the body which, shortly after birth, lose their ability to ever reduplicate themselves. These cells are located in the smooth muscle, skeletal muscle, heart muscle, kidney glomeruli, and nervous system.

Scar Formation

During the healing of a wound it is very important that the removal of exudate and dead cells take place. This is accomplished by phagocytes, which engulf the dead cells, and by the action of enzymes.

After the wound has been "cleansed" of dead cells and exudate, then further healing can take place. When too much of the skin is destroyed the defect is filled in by granulation tissue. The epithelium makes an attempt to migrate over the defect but is unable to cover it all. Thus, the granulation tissue fills the gap. As healing progresses the granulation tissue regresses, leaving a scar where the epithelium was not able to cover.

The chief component of scar tissue is collagen. Collagen is a protein molecule, which is made up of approximately one thousand amino acids. The electron microscope reveals that the collagen fibers have bumps and grooves in their structure. These permit an interlocking of the collagen fibers with each other. It is a lock-and-key arrangement. The bond between the fibrils of the collagen grows stronger as the wound heals. Collagen is not water-soluble and is also very resistant to chemical attack. These characteristics of collagen permit the underlying structures to be protected.

Factors Influencing Healing

There are several factors that affect wound healing. Age is one. A young person heals faster than an elderly person. Warmth, ultraviolet light, and good nutrition are very important factors in influencing a more rapid rate of wound healing. Experimentally it has been found that the feeding of zinc sulfate will accelerate wound healing in both man and animals.

Some of the factors that will delay wound healing are vitamin C deficiency, protein deficiency, steroid therapy, ionizing radiation, and diabetes. Psychological factors can also influence the rate of healing. A good positive mental attitude always promotes healing.

It is evident that the healing process was designed by the Creator. How could such a mechanism evolve? Many of the body systems are involved in the process of healing. The vascular system has to be present to carry the blood supply and nutrition to the healing area. Phagocytes are needed for cleaning up the wound and protection against infection. The nervous system keeps us alert and keeps us from reinjuring the area that is undergoing the process of healing.

The healing process is a mechanism of protection and defense. It also involves a backup system when scar formation takes place. A backup system is used when the primary system is unable to perform completely or only partially. Backup systems are designed-in systems made by the Creator. When the epithelial cells fail to cover over the wound area, the backup system of scar formation takes over.

Immunity

We hear a lot about immunity these days. The immunity with which we are concerned is the ability of an individual to resist the development of a disease. We will discuss both natural and acquired immunity.

Natural Immunity

Natural immunity is inborn or innate immunity. It also can be defined as inherited immunity or native immunity. Natural immunity is not to be confused with naturally acquired immunity. Certain pathogens (bacteria or viruses) have species specificity. For example, humans get mumps but dogs and cats never do. Amphibians have natural resistance to tetanus and diphtheria. It is not clearly understood why one species contracts a certain disease while another species has natural immunity to it. The body temperature of an animal is a factor in whether the animal contracts a certain disease or not. Chickens will become susceptible to anthrax if their body temperatures are lowered from 39°C to 37°C.

Race is another factor that influences natural immunity. Studies in this area are only valid when the environment is the same for all persons involved. This would include such places as prisons, mental hospitals, and military service. Under these circumstances it has been found that blacks are more susceptible to tuberculosis than whites, but blacks are more resistant to diphtheria and influenza than whites. (See books by Barrett and Gordon.)

Sex difference is also a factor in susceptibility or resistance to a certain disease. In laboratory experiments it has been found that female mice are more resistant to mouse typhoid than male mice, and females are more susceptible to fowl malaria than males.

Nutrition is another important factor that influences

resistance to disease. Generally speaking, good nutrition means better health and more resistance to infections. The contradiction to this is that a good diet may cause a greater susceptibility to viral disease. A nutritionally healthy cell will produce more viruses than a nutritionally depleted cell when they are invaded by a virus.

Hormonal imbalance, as in diabetes, can increase the susceptibility of an individual to infectious disease.

There are miscellaneous factors that influence natural immunity including age, climate, fatigue, mental health, and many others.

Passively Acquired Immunity

The immunity that an unborn child receives from its mother is passively acquired immunity. The antibodies produced by the mother are transported through the placenta into the unborn child's blood stream. Breast-fed infants also receive antibodies by way of the colostrum into the infant's gastrointestinal tract. These antibodies may ward off intestinal infections of the infant's digestive tract or they may be absorbed into the infant's blood stream. Bottle-fed babies do not have this protection.

There is also passively acquired immunity by artificial means. For example, an individual can be injected with small amounts of tetanus toxoid over a period of time. This individual will then develop a hyperimmune serum to the tetanus toxoid. When one who has not been immunized for tetanus has a wound, such as from sticking a nail in his foot, he needs treatment to prevent tetanus from developing. He can be given antibodies produced by another individual to prevent tetanus from developing. (Horse serum is no longer used for this purpose.) The antibodies produced by another individual are given by injection to the patient. These antibodies are specific for the tetanus toxin produced by the bacillus, Clostridium tetani.

Actively Acquired Immunity

Actively acquired immunity may be naturally acquired when an individual survives an infection. The immunity he receives from the infection may protect him partially or completely for the remainder of his life. However, since many diseases may result in death, this is not the best way to develop immunity.

By the use of vaccines and toxoids, actively acquired immunity may be produced by artificial means. This results in immunity without the individual getting sick.

No Immunity

Some interesting experiments have been done on humoral immunity in chickens. The lymphoid organ of the hindgut of neonatal chickens was removed, resulting in severe impairment of the antibody immune system. Nonetheless, the cellular immunity of the chickens seemed to be normal. A congenital sex-linked disease found in human male infants is practically identical to that produced in these chickens experimentally. Affected children, however, do not have an antibody response to infections.

Under normal circumstances the body doesn't produce any immune reaction to its own tissues. This is important, for otherwise there would be damage of our tissues from these immune responses. The body immune system has self-recognition of its own body tissues. It is not fully understood how this takes place, but it must occur early in the embryonic life of each individual.

Can you imagine how such an elaborate immune system could have evolved from lower forms of animal life? The immune response of the horse is so different from that of a human being that it is a dangerous thing to inject a patient with horse serum to prevent tetanus. The antibodies produced by a horse act as a foreign agent when injected into a human being for our protection against tetanus.

The rejection of organ transplants is due to the response of the recipient's immune system. The transplanted organ acts as a foreign tissue to the immune system. An organ transplant from an identical twin to his identical twin sister or brother is the only type of transplant that is never rejected.

Isn't it reasonable to believe that the uniqueness of each individual's system had to have been instantly created? The very fact that each of us has a different immune system is evidence for instant creation. Why should the immune systems of all animals be different, as well as differences within the species? The immune system is different for each individual unless he or she has an identical twin.

Any defect in the humoral immune system's response can result in death. This in itself is evidence that the immune system could not have waited millions of years to develop. The humoral immune system is a complicated biochemical mechanism. Its built-in self-recognition had to have been planned by a Creator. If the immune system did not have the built-in self-recognition it would destroy the normal tissues of our body. This is what happens to a patient who receives an organ transplant from a nonidentical twin donor.

Except for identical twins, each human being is genetically unique. If the immune system evolved, why is each individual unique? In order to get variety and individuality, the Creator made us biochemically different.

Protection and Defense

Most of us go about our daily routines never taking notice of our body's protection and defense systems. The reflex protection mechanisms are under the control of the nervous system. A normal person never worries about them. Suppose someone sticks out a foot and trips him. Immediately his emergency protection system comes into action. This is the extensor protective reflex system. His head would extend backward, his upper extremities extend, and he would land safely on the palms of his hands.

Can you imagine this marvelous reflex protective system that humans have today evolving from lower forms of life? Before the extensor protective mechanism evolved, how did our ancestors protect themselves from falls? This system had to be instantly created for our protection against trauma.

One of the first lessons we are taught in physiology is the withdrawal reflex. Have you ever accidentally touched something very hot? You immediately pulled your hand away. You did not continue to touch the hot area and take the time to think, "I must pull my hand away." Your automatic withdrawal reflex reacted immediately. It involves the following: (1) the receptor, which is the peripheral sensory nerve ending, (2) the transmitter, which is the nerve fiber that conducts the impulse to the spinal cord, and (3) the effector, which is the nerve fiber that goes to the muscles to stimulate them to contract and pull the hand away.

How do you suppose this reflex mechanism, that exists not only in man but in lower forms of life to protect against extreme temperatures, evolved? Did the hot temperatures of the desert cause this reflex to evolve? Before man was around to build fires, did forest fires caused by lightning cause this reflex to develop in lower forms of animal life? I am sure that all present-day, living polar bears have this reflex; why have they not lost it since they live in a very cold climate and have no use for it? The protective reflexes described above had to have been instantly created within each animal. Since some of these protective reflexes are seldom used, how could they have evolved when there are so few instances in which they are necessary? Shouldn't this protective reflex against heat become degenerate or completely absent in the polar bear, who has little or no use for it?

Instant creation is the only explanation for these marvelous protective reflex mechanisms.

White Blood Cells

No human soldier can match the bravery of a white blood cell. These microscopic soldiers never consider rank, pay, or recognition for their service, but will fight the causes of disease to their death. They never receive medals for the supreme sacrifices they make for us every day of our lives.

Where do the white blood cells come from? Early in embryonic life there is a development of sites where blood formation takes place. After two months of intra-uterine life, the liver of the fetus then takes over as the main site of the production of blood cells. During the seventh month of intra-uterine life the bone marrow will become the main source of production of blood cells and will continue to be for the remainder of our lives.

The most important white blood cell is the neutrophil. These tiny cells protect us against bacterial invasion. It is believed that when a tissue is damaged, it releases a chemical substance that attracts the white blood cells. These tiny fighters move from the blood vessel into the tissue to surround the invader.

The damaged tissue also produces a substance that is called the leukocytosis promoting factor. After this substance diffuses into the blood stream it causes the blood marrow to release white blood cells to go to the damaged tissue, where there is an immediate need for their service.

Each of these brave little fighters of the body can digest from 5 to 25 bacteria before it becomes exhausted and dies. The ingestion of only one or two very virulent bacteria may cause the death of a neutrophil.

One of the most amazing things to observe in a patient who has recently been in an accident is the rapid rise in the white blood cell count, as this defense mechanism goes into action. The white blood cell count can rise three to four times that of normal within an hour after an accident.

The Kupffer cells line the minute sinuses of the liver. These cells cleanse the blood from the intestinal tract before it enters into general circulation. The Kupffer cells are very effective in removing bacteria from the blood stream.

The many protective and defensive mechanisms of the body are too numerous to elaborate upon here. These protective and defensive mechanisms had to be working and ready to go at whatever levels of lower forms of life they became necessary.

The Coughing and Vomiting Reflexes

The act of coughing is initiated through the cough reflex. Coughing will result when there is mechanical stimulation to the mucosal linings of the tracheobronchial tree. A nerve impulse travels by way of the vagus nerve to the medulla. This information is transferred by numerous synapses to nerves that supply the muscles involved in coughing, which include the muscles that open the mouth, and the muscles of the rib cage, the diaphragm, and the abdomen.

The cough reflex is a protective mechanism. For example, a person who smokes frequently complains of "smoker's cough." In this case, the cough reflex is telling the smoker there is an irritation of the tracheobronchial tree. The cough reflex can also be set off by chemical irritants, infections, or mechanical obstructions.

Most of us have experienced a small particle of food or liquid "going down the wrong way," initiating the cough reflex. Under normal circumstances, a person does not go around coughing continually. Rather, the cough reflex is used for our protection in cases of emergency. This must have been the Creator's intention. Can you imagine such an elaborate system as the cough reflex mechanism just evolving? This reflex defies the evolutionist's explanation of slow evolvement due to environmental factors. It had to have been available and ready to go as each individual was born.

Vomiting Reflex

The vomiting reflex mechanism comes into action when there is irritation of the stomach, gall bladder, or gastrointestinal tract. Persons who have renal colic or appendicitis may also have stimulation of the vomiting reflex. Pungent disagreeable odors, disgusting sights, and motion sickness may also cause stimulation of the vomiting reflex.

For example, if there is irritation of the stomach, the receptor fibers of the vagus nerve transmit an impulse to the tractus solitarius of the medulla. This information is transferred to a rather complex system, which sends a message as follows: (1) The glottis is closed, (2) the nasopharynx is closed off by the elevation of the soft palate, preventing the vomited material from going into the nose, (3) contractions of the diaphragm and abdominal muscles follow, and (4) the muscles of the stomach and the esophagus relax. The strong contractions of the diaphragm and the abdominal muscles cause the stomach to be emptied under pressure from without, aided by the contraction of the lower portion of the stomach, which helps in the expulsion of the contents from the stomach. Sometimes in intestinal obstructions, reverse peristalsis will cause the intestinal contents to move upwards (or backwards) into the stomach and then be vomited out.

Parents of young children can make use of the vomiting reflex. When a young child has swallowed a large quantity of aspirin or nonvaporous poison, this reflex can become lifesaving. The parent can turn the child upside down and tickle the back of his throat, initiating the vomiting reflex. Sometimes the child will vomit because of the irritation produced by the poison itself on the gastrointestinal tract.

The coughing reflex and the vomiting reflex are closely associated. People frequently ask, "Why do I vomit when I cough?" This sometimes happens to those who have sore throats.

Undoubtedly, the Creator gave us this protective mechanism for a useful purpose. It is very unpleasant to vomit, but it is more unpleasant to be sick for a longer period of time. It is even worse to die because one has not vomited up a poison. I am sure that many have survived because of the vomiting reflex.

Ponder this question: How could environmental factors have caused the vomiting reflex to have evolved?

The Unborn's Protection and Defense

As a physician, I am awed by the wisdom of our Creator. Only by an intellect superior to a human being's could elaborate systems for protection and defense of the unborn have been designed.

Amniotic Fluid

The amniotic cavity is the dwelling place of the unborn. The embryo is suspended within this cavity by the umbilical cord, which is connected to the placenta. This enclosed cavity is filled with amniotic fluid, which has been produced by the amniotic cells. This fluid is essential for the protection of the unborn. It protects the fetus from injury. Pascal's Law is applicable here, since pressure applied to an enclosed fluid is transmitted equally in all directions.

Amniotic fluid also prevents adherence of the embryo to the amnion. This, in turn, permits freedom of movement of the fetus within the amniotic cavity. During childbirth amniotic fluid is essential. The membranes surrounding the fluid bulge down into the lower portion of the uterus. The pressure from the fluid helps to dilate the cervix of the uterus.

Today, students are still being told that amniotic fluid is reminiscent of our past. It is supposed to suggest the sea or primitive pond in which our ancestors once lived. None are so blind as those who will not see. We did not come from the sea.

What prevents an excessive amount of amniotic fluid from forming? In about the fifth month of its life, the fetus begins to swallow some of the amniotic fluid. Proof that the fetus is swallowing amniotic fluid is found in the gut tract, where lanugo hair is found in the contents of the fetus' intestine. If the fetus has a constricture of its esophagus it is unable to swallow amniotic fluid. This results in an excessive amount of amniotic fluid in the uterus, which will then be enlarged during the later stages of pregnancy.

It is difficult to determine how much fetal urinary secretions contribute to the amount of amniotic fluid produced. It is not unusual for a newborn infant to urinate immediately after delivery. A newborn male infant will urinate, frequently aiming the urine stream right into the doctor's face. It almost seems to be intentional. This in itself shows that the urinary system is functioning and able to contribute its part in starting the newborn infant out on a normal healthy life.

Umbilical Cord

During the rapid development of the intestinal loops, some of them are found in the coelomic space, which is in the umbilical cord. These intestinal loops are then pulled into the body of the embryo at the end of the third month of fetal life. The umbilical cord serves as a passage for the umbilical vessels, which go from the placenta into the body of the embryo. The vessels within the umbilical cord are not straight and rigid but are in a coil-like structure, surrounded by protective jelly. The cord is quite elastic in nature, and this serves to protect the lumen of the vessels, thus insuring a free flow of blood. It also permits freedom of movement of the fetus.

Immediately after birth has taken place, the cord is clamped off. The elasticity of the jelly and the vessels now aids in the rapid constriction and contraction of the vessels that are in the cord.

Placenta

The placenta serves as an "exchange post" between the maternal and fetal blood streams. The placenta's primary functions are: (1) the exchange of oxygen and carbon dioxide, (2) the supply of nutrients in the form of amino acid, glucose, vitamins, minerals, etc., (3) the exchange of the products of metabolism of the fetus into the maternal blood stream, and (4) the production of hormones.

It is believed that the placenta also serves as a barrier against certain diseases, and it is the place of transmission of maternal antibodies into the fetal blood stream. The fetus is supplied with maternal antibodies that protect it from certain infections, such as diphtheria, smallpox, and measles.

Each year we honor our mothers on Mother's Day. This is a good thing. Do you think that the Creator of the amniotic fluid, umbilical cord, and the placenta should also be honored?

The time from conception to birth is approximately nine months. Isn't this instant creation, when compared to the billions of years evolutionists believe it took for man to evolve?

7

The Decay and Death of the
Various Systems of the Body

It is necessary to review the laws of thermodynamics in our
study of the decay and death of the body's systems. The first
law of thermodynamics states that energy is neither created
nor destroyed. The second law of thermodynamics states that
all matter and energy tend toward a state of randomness or
disorder. The third law of thermodynamics states that at
absolute zero temperature the atoms of a crystal would be in
absolute perfect order. In other words, the third law of
thermodynamics is perfect order whereas the second law of
thermodynamics tends toward disorder.

The second law of thermodynamics is easily recognizable
from our earliest childhood. Every normal child sooner or
later discovers the law of gravity on his own. Likewise, the
child becomes aware of the law of decay and death. Each
discovers these laws long before he attends science classes in
school. Do you remember asking some of the following
questions when you were a child: Does everything that goes
up come down? Does everything die? Why do old people get
old? Why do people get sick and die?

Decay and Death

At an early age we all learn that decay and death are
inevitable. This is the working of the second law of thermodynamics. It is for this reason that physicians are needed.

The aging process, disease, and trauma assist in the working of the second law of thermodynamics. How? Every human being is vulnerable to the processes that lead to decay and death.

Another way of stating the second law of thermodynamics is that everything breaks down or eventually wears out. Everything goes from the complex to the less complex. This change is called entropy.

Aging

Aging or senescence is the deteriorative change that takes place within an organism as it grows older. The aging process is observed in all levels of life. The aging process has even been observed in fish. As male fish grow older there is a loss of reproductive capacity and an increase in abnormalities among their offspring. Male fish undergo senescence at an earlier age than the females. Fish that grow the fastest also age the fastest.

Progeria (Hutchinson-Gilford Syndrome) is a rare type of syndrome, which is believed to be transmitted by an autosomal recessive gene. This inherited disorder has been reported to have been found in siblings and first cousins. The child has a normal birth but stops growing early in life and premature aging takes place. There is shortness of stature, a loss of subcutaneous fat, and a birdlike appearance of the face. The head appears large in comparison to the face. The chin is small and receding. There is a loss of hair from the scalp, eyebrows, and eyelashes. The skin looks old and wrinkly. There are degenerative changes of the bones, heart, and central nervous system. The blood cholesterol is also increased. Those suffering from Progeria may have coronary or cerebral vascular occlusions early in life. (See figure 7.1 of a child with this inherited disorder.)

Any Exceptions to Decay and Death?

The evolutionists teach that there were enough good mutations to permit man to evolve from lower forms of life.

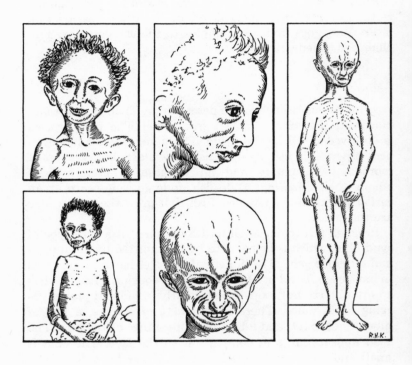

Fig. 7.1. Progeria (Hutchinson-Gilford Syndrome). Photographs 1, 2, and 3 are of the same boy. Photographs 4 and 5 are of another boy with progeria. *Courtesy of Dr. Sidney Gellis, from* Atlas of Mental Retardation Syndromes *by Sidney Gellis, Murray Feingold, and Joel Rutman.*

This is simply not true, as this discussion of the decay and death of the various systems of the body reveals.

Overwhelming evidence shows that there is a breakdown of the genetic system as well as other systems of the body. The second law of thermodynamics is responsible for the inherited genetic disorders of man. Every system of the body is affected. There are inherited disorders that cause blindness, deafness, mental retardation, congenital heart disease, liver disease, kidney disease, inborn errors of metabolism, and many other inherited diseases too numerous to elaborate on.

The evolutionist does not accept the second law of thermodynamics because he wants to save face. These evolutionists are not educated enough in human or animal pathology to realize that their findings are due to congenital abnormalities. Some almost go into a state of shock when they are confronted with this viewpoint.

We know that certain congenital malformations can be reproduced in animals by feeding them certain types of plants, or by virus injections.

Suppose someone has a superficial laceration of the arm. Under normal circumstances, without the aid of any medical assistance, the healing process will take place. Is this healing process breaking the second law of thermodynamics? The healing process is designed into the body by the Creator. It could be considered a temporary overruling of the second law of thermodynamics. This does not mean the person will live forever. If a wound is in a strategic area, death may ensue immediately.

The theory that man evolved from lower forms of life is not only unscientific, it is ridiculous. The genetic system is subject to the law of decay and death.

Down's Syndrome (Mongolism)

Mongolism is congenital idiocy, which has appeared in medical literature for over a century. This mental retardation syndrome was described by Dr. J. Legdon Down in 1866, in a paper published in the London Hospital Reports. Down named it Mongolian Idiocy. Because of the racial implication of the term *mongolism,* the condition has also been referred to as Down's Syndrome or Down's Anomaly.

There are two separate descriptions of patients that suggest mongolism. One description was done by Sequin in 1846 and the other, ten years earlier, by Esquirol, in 1836. Mongolism has been reported among practically every racial group and in practically every country.

The incidence rate of Down's Syndrome at birth varies. The Europeans report that there is one mongoloid in every 700 births. In Australia the rate is practically the same, 1 in every 688 live births. Among Negroes, this rate is much lower, only 1 or 2 per 10,000 births. The rate of occurrence varies greatly with the age of the mother. If the mother's age is only 20 years, the incidence rate is only 1 in 2,300 live births. The rate of occurrence of mongoloid babies increases with age of the mother. In mothers who are 45 years and over the incidence rate of mongolism increases to 1 in 54.

Actually the incidence rate of Down's Syndrome at conception is much higher than the live birth rate. The reason for this is that there are many spontaneous abortions of the fetus in which there are chromosomal abnormalities. It has been estimated that there are 7.3 mongoloid fetuses in every 1,000 conceptions.

The following are clinical findings relating to mongolism.
• The head in mongolism is small, with a flattening of the posterior portion of the skull. The face also appears to be flat. In some mongoloids the head may even appear to be microcephalic (fig. 7.2).
• The ears may be abnormal in that the upper parts seem to flop down.
• In Down's Syndrome the eyes appear to be smaller than normal and also to have an epicanthic fold different from that seen in a normal oriental eye (fig. 7.3). The iris of a child with this syndrome also has speckled irides.
• The noses on mongoloid children appear to be very flat. There is no height in the bridge of the nose.

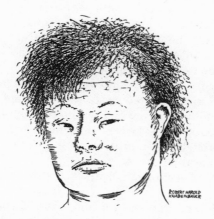

Fig. 7.2. Down's Syndrome (mongoloid). *Courtesy of Dr. Hazel Berglund.*

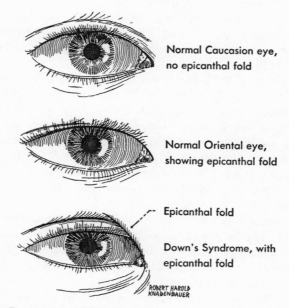

Normal Caucasion eye,
no epicanthal fold

Normal Oriental eye,
showing epicanthal fold

Epicanthal fold

Down's Syndrome, with
epicanthal fold

Fig. 7.3. Types of eye folds or shapes.

• Often the teeth are misshapen or fused. Even in mongoloid children who have had excellent care, the teeth often appear to lack good enamel formation and also to have some discoloration. Often there is a congenital absence of some of the deciduous teeth in the mongoloid child.

• The tongue of a mongoloid child often appears to be enlarged. (Some disagree with this finding.) Because the mongoloid child often has to breathe through his mouth, the tongue appears to be larger. It is not certain whether he breathes through his mouth because of habit or because of malformed nasal passages.

• The neck of a mongoloid always seems to be short and thick.

Mongoloid children have a high rate of congenital heart disease. During the first year of life there is high mortality among mongoloids with cardiac defects. In 1969, the parents of a mongoloid child with a congenital heart defect refused to have corrective cardiac surgery done on their infant. The case was taken to court and the parents won the case. The infant later died. In a medical genetics class, the students, as well as the medical genetics professor, felt that the parents had done the right thing.

The external genitalia of mongoloid male infants usually appear to be poorly developed. In adult males the pubic hair is invariably straight and silky, the axillary hair and beards thinly distributed. The sex drive of mongoloid males seems to be very much diminished, and there is a reduced sperm count in the semen. No mongoloid known has ever fathered a child. In females who are mongoloid menstruation is often absent. They have poorly developed breasts, and their pubic hair is very sparse.

The skin in mongoloid children often appears to be soft and babylike. The hair of the head is often very sparse and fine in texture. Some physicians believe that this may be due to a hypothyroid condition, which may also occur in mongols.

• Shortness of stature is another common feature of mongoloid children, who appear to be short and stocky. The trunk length in mongoloid adults is only slightly reduced in comparison to that of normal adults. Their shortness is primarily due to the marked reduction in the length of the lower extremities. There is also a decrease in length of their upper extremities. This shortness of stature cannot be attributed to poor nutrition.

• The hand of a mongoloid is usually very broad with short stubby fingers, and may contain only one transverse palmar crease.

• The feet are short and wide with short stubby toes.

• Muscle tone is lacking in the mongoloid infant. This may account for its delayed ability to sit, stand, or walk.

• Some reports give the I.Q. range of the majority of mongoloids as being below 25, which is the idiot range. Others feel that the majority of mongoloids are imbeciles with I.Q.'s of 25 to 49. This low intelligence is the saddest finding of all.

Genetic Pathology

Under normal circumstances, in man, there are 46 chromosomes. There are 22 pairs of nonsex chromosomes that are called autosomes. XY are the sex chromosomes of a normal male. XX are the normal sex chromosomes of a female.

In Down's Syndrome the laboratory findings show an extra chromosome. There are 47 chromosomes instead of the normal 46. In the majority of cases, chromosome pair 21 is 3 instead of 2. (See figure 7.4, the diagram of this genetic disaster resulting in a Down's Syndrome.)

Space does not permit a full discussion of all the chromosomal abnormalities associated with mongoloidism. Unfortunately there are known cases of familial mongoloidism. When one parent has a translocation of a pair of chromosomes, which are completely stuck together, the result is mongolism. Normally, in the gonad, there is a reduction of the number of chromosomes by one-half in both the ovum and sperm. If a parent has a pair of chromosomes that are stuck together, he or she will produce all mongoloid children, even though he or she is perfectly normal. (See figure 7.5, the diagram of a pair of normal chromosomes, and compare it with a pair of stuck chromosomes or translocated chromosomes.)

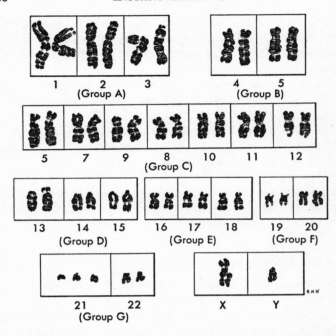

Fig. 7.4. Chromosome analysis. Modal number 47 with XY complement and an extra-small chromosome consistent with the G(21-22) group. In support of the clinical impression, this chromosome pattern is consistent with "Trisomy 21" Down's Syndrome (mongolism) in an XY male. *Courtesy of Dr. W. R. Centerwall, Director, Genetics, Birth Defects and Chromosome Services, Loma Linda University Medical Center.*

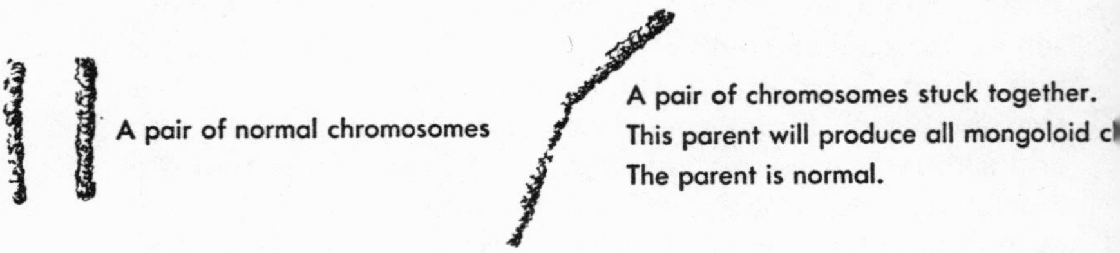

A pair of normal chromosomes

A pair of chromosomes stuck together. This parent will produce all mongoloid c The parent is normal.

Fig. 7.5. Chromosomes that will produce mongoloid children.

It is believed that from 10 to 15 percent of all pregnancies terminate in spontaneous abortion. Studies of the aborted specimens reveal that many of them had chromosomal abnormalities.

Mongolism Associated with Other Diseases

Epidemiological studies have shown an increased rate of mongoloids developing leukemia. Leukemia has also been reported among family members of mongoloids.

Mongolism and thyroid disease are also associated. Mongoloids may have either hypothyroidism or hyperthyroidism. Mongolism is also associated with other chromosomal abnormalities, which will be discussed later.

Prevention of Mongolism

It would be advisable for anyone with a mongoloid relative or a mongoloid child to have a genetic study done before he or she has a child. Since the risk of mongolism greatly increases with age, it is advisable for such persons, particularly women, not to have children after the age of 35.

Some medical geneticists have suggested that any woman who is pregnant in the older age group should have an amniocentesis, in which the cells in the amniotic fluid are examined for chromosomal abnormalities. If the diagnosis of mongolism is made, the prospective mother then has the choice of either having a mongoloid child or having an abortion.

Down's Syndrome is evidence of a breakdown in the genetic system. This is not evolution, going from a lower state to a higher state, but devolution, which is degeneration.

Phenylketonuria (PKU)

Phenylketonuria is commonly referred to by physicians as PKU. PKU is an inborn error of metabolism. In general a disease is any departure from the state of health; therefore, PKU can be considered an inherited disease.

In 1934, Dr. Asbjorn Folling, Professor of Nutritional Research at the University of Oslo School of Medicine, was checking retarded children for chronic infections. He found none. Since Dr. Folling was trained as a biochemist as well as a physician, he decided to do some chemical analyses on the urine of these retarded children. He tested the urine for acetoacetic acid, which is an end product of fat metabolism. This acid is found in people who have been on a prolonged fast or who have uncontrolled diabetes. When 10 percent ferric chloride is added to urine that has acetoacetic acid, a red-brown color appears. But the urine of some of the retarded children turned green when tested. Dr. Folling then made an effort to extract the product or products that caused the green color. He found it to be phenylpyruvic acid. Dr. Folling concluded that there was a good possibility that some of these retarded children had a disturbance in their metabolism of phenylalanine, which is an amino acid. He reasoned that this could be the cause of the mental retardation of these children. Dr. Folling found ten cases of mental retardation in which there was disturbance in their metabolism of phenylalanine. Two of these children were siblings.

Dr. Folling published a report of his findings (see Frank Lyman) of an inherited disorder of phenylalanine metabolism. He called this syndrome *imbecilitas phenylpyruvica.*

Since the great majority of children born with PKU are severely mentally retarded, they are usually found in institutions for the mentally deficient.

Many countries have reported cases of PKU, including most of the countries of western Europe, the United States, Canada, Australia, New Zealand, Poland, and even Japan.

PKU is most often found in Americans of European origin. It is believed to be transmitted by a recessive autosomal gene. The syndrome only makes its appearance in a newborn infant when the child has inherited an abnormal gene from each of his or her parents. There are reports of rare, untreated phenylketonuric individuals who have near normal intelligence.

The incidence of PKU is one in 20,000 live births.

The biochemical explanation for PKU is a lack of a specific liver enzyme, which is used in the metabolism of phenylalanine. It is believed that in PKU the phenylpyruvic acid inhibits oxygen consumption in the brain, resulting in a lack of brain development. Obviously, this results in mental retardation.

There are other manifestations of the PKU syndrome. Untreated PKU patients may also have epilepsy, muscular hypertonicity, motor impairment, small body size, skin lesions, and defects in pigmentation. Affected children also may be very sensitive to sunlight.

There is one redeeming factor concerning this syndrome. PKU can be prevented by a phenylalanine-restricted diet. Most hospitals routinely check the urine of newborn infants for this metabolic defect. Because it is such a simple test, it can be done after the mother and child return to their physician for follow-up care. The test is not always positive immediately after birth, and may not be positive until the thirty-fourth day of the infant's life.

The accompanying picture (fig. 7.6) of an 11-year-old boy with PKU, who is obviously mentally retarded, contrasts his appearance with that of his two-and-a-half-year-old sister, who is normal. She was treated with a phenylalanine-restricted diet.

PKU is an inherited error of metabolism. A restricted diet for PKU children will prevent mental retardation. The physician cannot change the inherited genes that the PKU child has, but he can restrict the diet, allowing the PKU child to have normal mental development.

One would have to conclude that the recessive gene for PKU is a bad gene. When an infant is born having a pair of these recessive deleterious genes, he has PKU. This is obviously not an upward step in the process of evolution.

Fig. 7.6. Contrast the difference between an untreated severely retarded 11-year-old boy and his normal 2½-year-old sister, who was treated for PKU. *Courtesy of Dr. W. R. Centerwall, Pediatrics Dept., Loma Linda University.*

Muscular Dystrophy

Muscular dystrophy is actually a group of primary diseases of muscles of several different clinical types. The genetic patterns of these muscular dystrophies may be the dominant type, simple recessive type, or sex-linked type.

The most common type of muscular dystrophy is referred to as the Duchenne type, after the man who described it in 1868. The disease is due to an X-linked recessive gene. This recessive gene in males acts in a dominant way, because males only have one X chromosome, which is paired up with their Y chromosome. Female carriers rarely show any clinical symptom of this muscular disorder.

Muscular weakness is the chief symptom of affected children. The gluteal muscles are involved first, which results in a child's falling easily and then having difficulty in getting up again (fig. 7.7).

Muscular involvement is usually symmetrical. As more of the muscles are involved, the child becomes confined to a wheelchair or bed.

The prognosis for this disease is lethal. It is estimated that three-fourths of the cases of Duchenne's muscular dystrophy die before the age of twenty. Patients with this disease usually die of respiratory infections or cardiac failure, or both.

• Microscopic examinations reveal a marked variation in the size of the muscle fibers. As the disease progresses more of the muscle is replaced by fat and connective tissue. In this instance, fat power cannot replace muscle power.

• The electromyogram in Duchenne's disease shows abnormal potentials that indicate degeneration of the muscle fibers. About 25 percent of all patients also have abnormal electrocardiograms. It has been found that the creatinine phosphokinase, which is a muscle enzyme, may be elevated fifty- to a hundredfold in children just prior to the onset of their symptoms of muscular weakness. This serum enzyme gradually decreases to normal, but may again become elevated in later stages of this disease. It has been shown that 80 percent of all female carriers show a borderline or a slight increase in the elevation of the serum creatinine phosphokinase.

This dreadful disease is caused by a mutant gene, which shows evidence of decay of the muscular system due to bad mutation. This is evidence that a change in the genetic system is not for the advancement of the human race. It reaps misery and death.

In one family of four boys and two girls who have suffered the emotional, as well as the physical, effects of this disease, one son is already dead, two teenage boys are advancing toward their terminal end, and one thirteen-year-old boy so far appears to be normal. The normal son has not shown any increase in his serum creatinine phosphokinase. The two girls in the family have already married and reproduced children.

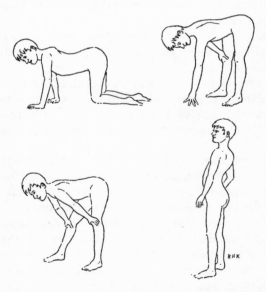

Fig. 7.7. A boy with muscular dystrophy showing the difficulty of rising from the floor due to muscular weakness.

The father of the affected boys stated that his daughters disregarded genetic counseling not to have children.

Sickle Cell Anemia

Sickle cell anemia is a genetic defect of the Negro race. It is believed that there are about 30,000 people in the United States who suffer from it and another 1.5·million who carry the sickle cell trait.

Sickle cell anemia is an inherited, molecular disease that manifests itself in the malformation of the hemoglobin molecule. During the process in which hemoglobin is made, there is a substitution of valine amino acid for glutamic amino acid. This abnormality occurs in the hemoglobin formation of the sickle cell. The substitution of a valine amino acid causes a stacking of the hemoglobin molecules in the red blood cells, which then results in sickling of the cell. It occurs when the oxygen is released in the capillaries of the tissues.

A child born with sickle cell anemia may show clinical manifestations as early as the second or third month of life. It has been estimated that from 30 to 50 percent of all affected children show some clinical symptoms by the time they are one year of age.

Those suffering from the disease often have a slender build and long legs. They frequently complain of severe pain in the abdomen and in the legs, and have severe pain in their joints, which are hot and swollen. Frequently, they have thrombosis of many small vessels, which may result in convulsions, coma, bone infarctions, leg ulcers, and necrosis of the femoral head. They may also have enlargement of the spleen, cardiac involvement, gallstones, and recurring blood in the urine.

• The treatment is primarily symptomatic. If the disease causes a crisis, the patient may need transfusions.

• The prognosis for these patients, needless to say, is not good. Death can result from cerebral, cardiac, or hemolytic complications. Since renal damage is very common, death may result from uremia. There are fewer crises as the patient advances in age, and some live to be over fifty years of age.

• The patient with sickle cell disease has a homozygous for the sickling gene. This individual has inherited a gene from each parent that makes him have an inherited defect in the production of the hemoglobin of his red blood cells. Those who have a sickle cell trait have a heterozygous genotype. They are usually asymptomatic. They have a normal peripheral blood count. No sickling is seen in the peripheral blood smear. The sickle cell trait can be demonstrated by an incubation of the red blood cells by sodium metabisulfate.

One of the primary jobs of the spleen is to filter out defective, misshapen, and old red blood cells of the blood system and salvage the iron and protein from these cells for reuse in the production of new red blood cells. The misshapen sickled cells are primary targets for destruction by the spleen.

It is true that persons who have sickle cell anemia are more resistant to malaria. This does not mean that the genetic defect of sickled cells was brought about by the malaria parasite in previous generations.

The malaria parasite must have a healthy, normal-shaped red blood cell to invade and to be able to grow and reproduce in. The sickled red blood cell is not sturdy enough to survive this type of invasion by the malaria parasite.

Compare the drawing (fig. 7.8) of the blood smear of sickled cells with the blood smears of normal red blood cells. As you can see, the malaria parasite needs a normal-shaped red blood cell for invasion and survival.

Other congenital defects also prevent disease. I have never known a patient with inherited deafness to complain about ringing in the ears. Patients with congenital absence of the lower extremities can never have gangrene of the big toe.

Marfan's Syndrome

In 1896, Marfan's original report described the syndrome that bears his name. This syndrome comes under the classification of hereditary disorder of connective tissue.

• Individuals with this syndrome are very tall and thin with a noticeable lack of subcutaneous fat. Their extremities are long and thin; their fingers are referred to as "spider fingers." Spinal curvatures and deformities of the chest are also frequent features of Marfan's Syndrome, as are loose joints. A patient with Marfan's Syndrome can often reach around his back to the opposite side and then go in front of the abdomen and touch his umbilicus. This is achieved by his long extremities and the looseness of his joints.

Eye defects are common. Sometimes there is displacement of the lens, sometimes detachment of the retina. Myopia may also be present along with other ocular abnormalities.

• Because of weaknesses in the walls of the great vessels, there may be dilatation that can result in dissecting aneurysms, which are frequently fatal. Aneurysms may develop as early as the first two years of life or not until the

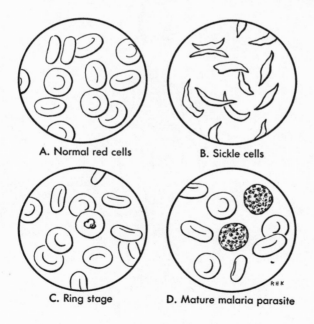

A. Normal red cells   B. Sickle cells

C. Ring stage   D. Mature malaria parasite

Fig. 7.8. Drawings from blood smears. *Courtesy of Loma Linda University, Hematology Dept. and Microbiology Dept.*

patient is in his forties or fifties. Involvement of the valves of the heart may lead to cardiac complications that will result in death. See figure 7.9, a photograph of a woman with Marfan's Syndrome. Note the long slender extremities and long slender fingers.

• Respiratory infections are common and are treated with appropriate antibiotics. Spinal deformities may be alleviated to some degree by bracing. The measures to be taken to correct any eye defects would have to be made by an ophthalmologist. The cardiovascular involvement may require more than just treatment for cardiac decompensation.

Can you think of a famous American who had this syndrome? Medical geneticists claim that Abraham Lincoln had Marfan's Syndrome. They also believe that the children

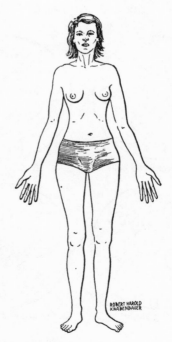

Fig. 7.9. Marfan's Syndrome.

he lost during their early childhood died as a result of
Marfan's Syndrome.
• Marfan's Syndrome is a dominant inherited genetic disorder that affects the connective tissue proteins of the body.
The defect may be in an incorrect amino acid sequence of the
collagen. A substitution of the wrong amino acids can cause
havoc, as was seen in the discussion of sickle cell anemia.

Isn't it reasonable to believe that the Creator gave Adam a
perfect genetic system that has undergone change? This
change is not an upward trend but definitely a downward
one. Marfan's Syndrome is a perfect example of this downward trend.

Dwarfs and Midgets

A person's final height is determined not only by genetic
factors, but also by environmental factors, such as poor
nutrition and even emotional deprivation.

Achondroplasia

A dwarf of the achondroplasia type has distinctive characteristics. The head is usually large, and may show the typical
clinical picture of an arrested hydrocephalus. Mental retardation may secondarily appear due to the hydrocephalus.
The forehead is usually bulging and the bridge of the nose is
usually depressed. The vertebral column of such dwarfs
makes the upper portion of the back look rounded. The lower
portion of the back has a swaybacked appearance.

Progressive paraplegia may result from malformed vertebrae. The curvatures of the spine will also cause protrusion
of the abdomen and the gluteal region. The extremities are
short and curved. (See fig. 7.10 for this type of dwarf.)

The pathology of this type of dwarfism is due to a
disturbance of the cartilaginous growth area of the bones,
which causes the bones of the extremities to be short, wide,
and dense.

Many affected children die in utero or shortly after birth. If there are no brain development complications due to hydrocephalus, they can develop a mental intelligence comparable to the inheritance they received from their parents. These dwarfs rarely reach a height above 55 inches. There is no specific treatment other than correction of developing deformities.

The mode of transmission of this genetic disorder is by a dominant autosomal inheritance. A more severe form may also appear as an autosomal recessive type. Many achondroplastic dwarfs have been found to have had a father of advanced age carrying a mutant gene. This type of dwarfism affects males and females equally.

Fig. 7.10. Achondroplasia type of dwarf.

Diastrophic Dwarfism

In this type of dwarfism the patient usually has a normal-sized head. He may have some malformation of the ears with ossification of the cartilages of the ear, and a cleft palate as well as the tendency to develop scoliosis. He is apt to have short extremities and club feet. His thumbs are proximally placed to give the appearance of what is termed "hitchhiker's thumb."

Because affected children have normal intelligence, all possible corrective measures should be taken.

The genetic etiology of this type of dwarfism is believed to be an autosomal recessive inheritance.

Pituitary Dwarfism

By definition there is a difference between a dwarf and a midget. A dwarf is a short person whose proportions are abnormal, whereas a midget is a short person whose proportions are normal.

Tom Thumb was a famous midget of the Barnum Circus in the latter half of the nineteenth century. His real name was Charles S. Stratton. Tom Thumb's father thought that his midget son was evidence of God's wrath against the Strattons. The real cause of Tom Thumb's shortness of stature was the deficiency of the growth hormone, which is produced by the pituitary gland.

Pituitary dwarfs usually have a youthful-looking face, infantile fat distribution, small hands and feet. They also have delayed sexual maturation.

An inbred religious sect has a group of six hypopituitary midgets. This group shows clinical manifestations of hypothyroidism and also adrenal insufficiency.

It is by radio-immunoassay that the amount of growth hormones in the blood stream are determined. Do the Pygmies of the Central Africa Republic have a growth hormone deficiency? The growth hormone blood assay of the

Pygmies' blood is normal, and further research is necessary to determine what causes the Pygmies' shortness of stature.

The genetic etiology of pituitary dwarfs is due to a pair of recessive genes, which produce a midget such as Tom Thumb. A child born from midget parents will also be a midget. Midget females who become pregnant must be delivered by Caesarean section.

Human pituitary hormone is not commercially available for the treatment of midgets.

Huntington's Chorea

Huntington's Chorea was first described by George Huntington in 1872. Huntington described the disease as having a hereditary tendency and a tendency toward insanity and suicide, and as first making its appearance during adult life. We now know that Huntington's Chorea may first make its clinical appearance as early as four or five years of age.

Psychological findings usually precede any neurological findings a physician would pick up on a neurological examination. Affected patients may become impulsive and antisocial in their behavior. Relatives of these unfortunates often recognize the symptoms long before a physical examination could demonstrate the manifestations of Huntington's Chorea. The onset of the disease usually comes between the ages of 20 and 45. Patients often complain of difficulty in speaking, with properly enunciating words. There may also be difficulty in the control of their eye movements. The most common clinical feature of this disease is chorea, or involuntary and irregular jerking movements of the limbs. At first the movements may be only slight jerking, purposeless movements, but as time progresses the movements become more frequent and more grotesque. The constant choreiform movement wears the patient out and only ceases during sleep. There is also marked mental deterioration. In from five to fifteen years the patient becomes totally bedridden.

There is no known biochemical test that can predict Huntington's Chorea. Electroencephalograms were done on individuals whose families had Huntington's Chorea, but no accurate predictions could be made as to which individuals would later develop Huntington's Chorea.

Autopsy shows that the brains are shrunken in size, and there is definite atrophy of the cortex of the brain, which caused the mental deterioration. The basal ganglia also show degeneration.

This neurological disease is transmitted by an autosomal dominant trait. Two brothers who came from England to America are the progenitors of many of the cases of Huntington's Chorea found in America. Although new mutations can occur, both the affected brothers have a strong family history that includes this tragic disease. Medical geneticists feel that carriers of this disease should refrain from reproduction. One of America's most talented country composer-singers died of Huntington's Chorea. His adult son has married and now has a child. Time will eventually tell what the future holds for these individuals.

This tragic disease causes degeneration and death of the nervous system.

Polycystic Kidney Disease

There are several different types of polycystic kidney disease, but this discussion will be concerned only with the two most common types, the adult form and the neonatal form.

Neonatal Form

The neonatal form of polycystic kidney disease may cause stillbirth. Large bilateral cystic kidneys of an unborn child can cause difficulties in delivery. Infants who survive delivery may live for a few months or up to two years, but they finally succumb to renal failure. Some of these children also have cystic malformations of other organs such as the liver, pancreas, lung, and brain. It is believed that the infantile type is transmitted by an autosomal recessive gene.

Adult Form

The usual time for the onset of the adult form of polycystic kidney disease is in the third or fourth decade of life; however, the onset of the first symptoms may be as early as eight or as late as 77 years of age. Those affected may have blood in the urine, pain due to clots, or acute kidney infections. There is often hypertension due to progressive renal failure. High blood pressure may cause strokes and cardiac failure, which may result in immediate death. The physician must institute treatment for kidney infections, kidney failure, hypertension, and heart failure.

Polycystic kidneys have a nodular surface because of the formation of large cysts. There is an obvious blockage of the urine so that it cannot reach the lower portion of the kidneys to eventually drain into the bladder and then be urinated. (Compare the drawings of the polycystic kidneys, fig. 7.11, with the smooth surface of normal kidneys.)

The adult form of polycystic kidney disease is inherited by an autosomal dominant gene. The genetic mutation that results is the cause of much suffering and pain.

Congenital Defects

Congenital defects are imperfections that are present at birth. They may be caused by inheritance, maternal infections during pregnancy, chromosomal abnormalities, maternal-fetal incompatibility, drugs, and other, unknown causes. Birth defects include structural as well as molecular deformities, such as sickle cell anemia. This section will discuss some of the abnormalities that may be present in the fetus or the newborn infant.

Defects of the Extremities

Polydactyly is duplication of one or more digits of the fingers or toes. Extra digits are often fused one with another and are frequently small in size. Polydactyly is found in many nationalities. Among the Amish people of Pennsylvania there are reports of cases of dwarfism accompanied by extra fingers, believed to have been transmitted by a simple recessive gene. The incidence of extra fingers in newborn infants in Uganda is reported to be as high as one in 74. One Arabic tribe, with a high frequency of polydactyly, killed any infant born with only five fingers. They believed that a normal infant was the result of adultery. Extra digits also have been reported among certain tribes of the Australian Aborigines. Polydactyly may also be associated with other congenital defects such as harelip and cleft palate. Most cases of polydactyly have been transmitted by a dominant inheri-

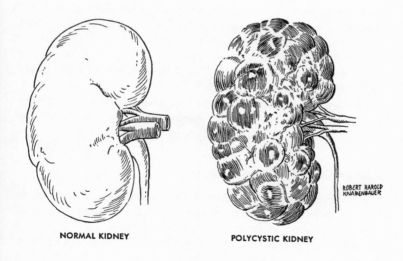

NORMAL KIDNEY   POLYCYSTIC KIDNEY

Fig. 7.11. Polycystic kidney contrasted with normal one.

tance, but some may be transmitted by a recessive inheritance.

This extra-digit congenital defect also may occur in fowls, rats, and domestic animals.

There is a high incidence of polydactyly in fetuses that have aborted spontaneously.

When an infant is born with the normal number of fingers, but there is fusion between the fingers, it is referred to as syndactyly. Usually this can be corrected by surgery. If the fingers are webbed together by skin, a zigzag incision can be made between the fingers. There is usually enough skin for one finger but the other finger must be skin-grafted. Sometimes these fingers are just a batch of bones and tendons, which makes it difficult for the surgeon to separate them into fingers.

Another defect of the hands and feet is referred to as lobster claws. This deformity involves split hands or split feet (see fig. 7.12). This trait is believed to be transmitted by a dominant gene.

An infant may also be born with the absence of one or both hands, or feet. Deformities of the extremities may vary greatly: the hands may be attached to the shoulders without arms; there may be a complete absence of the entire upper extremities; there may also be a complete absence of the lower extremities. Amelia is complete absence of both lower and upper extremities (see fig. 7.13).

Congenital dislocation of the hip, another defect that may be present at birth, may be suspected if the creases of the buttocks of a newborn infant are at different levels.

Cardiovascular Malformations

Malformations of the heart and vessels vary greatly in degree and in location. A patent ductus arteriosus is one of the more common forms of cardiovascular defect. It makes up about 10 percent of all cases of congenital heart defects. During fetal life the blood from the pulmonary artery is shunted into the aorta via a vessel called the ductus

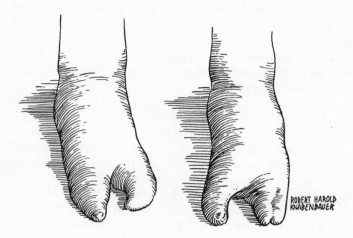

Fig. 7.12. Baby born with malformation of the feet called "lobster claw."

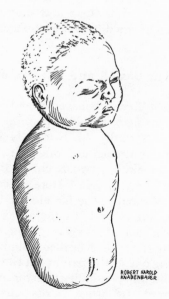

Fig. 7.13. Baby born without arms and legs.

arteriosus. Shortly after birth this vessel is supposed to decrease in size and form a fibrous band to shut off the flow of blood between the pulmonary artery and the aorta. If this does not happen, then the person has a patent ductus arteriosus. This congenital defect is more frequently found in females than in males.

Pyloric Stenosis

Pyloric stenosis is the narrowing of the lower portion of the stomach as it enters into the small intestine. This defect occurs in one of every 500 births and from three to four times more often in males than in females. The child usually vomits after each feeding, and there is a noticeable lack of gain in the infant's weight. X-ray findings will reveal a stringlike channel between the stomach and intestine. Surgery is necessary to relieve this condition.

It is certainly evident that birth defects are of no benefit to the individual who has them and that they are evidence of the breakdown of the different systems of the body.

The Sex (X and Y) Chromosomes

Up until 1956 it was believed that the normal number of chromosomes in man was 48. This number was found to be incorrect: it is actually 46. Normally we have 22 pairs of autosomal chromosomes and one pair of sex chromosomes. The normal female has two X chromosomes (XX), and the male one X and one Y (XY). Here we can see the wisdom of the Creator. Normally, the female produces one X chromosome in each ovum, and the male has either an X or a Y chromosome in each of his sperm. Thus, the sex of the child is determined by the male sperm containing either an X or a Y. By eliminating one of the parents in the determination of the sex of the child, the possibility of error in sex determination is greatly reduced. In other words, the chances of a hermaphrodite and other sexual chromosomal abnormalities are greatly reduced.

True Hermaphrodite

A true hermaphrodite has an XX and an XY combination. Individuals with this combination of chromosomes have fairly well differentiated ovary and testes. Their external genitalia are predominantly developed along the male line and they are, therefore, usually reared as males. The fallopian tube and uterus are present on the side where the ovary is found. During adolescence a hermaphrodite may develop gynecomastia (breasts), and menstruation may occur.

A true hermaphrodite may show some development of the testes, but the sperm count is very low and they are usually infertile. Although the ovaries are better developed, and the patient is able to menstruate, they are usually infertile. True hermaphrodites frequently have malignant tumors of the gonads.

The sex determination is usually made on the appearance of the external genitalia at birth. For instance, if the decision is made to rear the child as a male, the female gonad and ducts should be removed to avoid sex reversal at puberty. Since true hermaphrodites seldom produce enough of the sex hormone to produce the secondary sexual characteristics needed at puberty, they can be given hormone therapy.

Turner's Syndrome

Turner's Syndrome is a genetic disorder that occurs about once in every 3,000 births. Those with the disorder have only 45 chromosomes instead of the normal 46. This syndrome primarily involves the female. Instead of having XX chromosomes, she has only one X chromosome.

Affected infants are usually of low birth weight. There is webbing and shortness of the neck. Later on these children show shortness of stature, a low hair line, a receding chin, and a failure to develop sexually at puberty. They fail to develop breasts or pubic and axillary hair, and to menstruate. Their IQ is usually normal. They frequently have other congenital malformations involving the cardiovascular system, the urinary tract, and the skeletal system.

Turner's Syndrome has also been described in males, but the etiology is still unknown. Although chromosomal abnormalities have been found in some males with Turner's Syndrome, the majority of them have a normal male XY pair of sex chromosomes.

Since Turner's Syndrome primarily involves the female, psychic hormone therapy should be instituted about the age of thirteen or fourteen. Turner's Syndrome can be transmitted from affected mothers to one-half the daughters they have. (See fig. 7.14, the diagram describing this transmission of Turner's Syndrome.)

X X
NORMAL FEMALE

X Y
NORMAL MALE

OX female with Turner's Syndrome

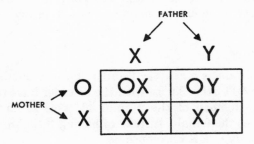

Fig. 7.14. Mother with Turner's Syndrome will produce half of daughters with the same defect. The OY is not viable.

Klinefelter's Syndrome

Klinefelter's Syndrome occurs in about one in a thousand male infants. The cause of this syndrome is the presence of an extra X chromosome. The most common form of chromosomal abnormality in this syndrome is designated as XXY. Some patients may have as high as six X chromosomes. Some may have more than one Y chromosome.

These individuals have small external genitalia. During puberty there is enlargement of the breasts, and due to the lack of production of testosterone, a slowing down in the development of male secondary sex characteristics. There is a noticeable lack of facial hair.

A low IQ is often found. Mental and physical abnormalities increase with the number of sex chromosomes. Klinefelter's Syndrome has been found in brothers. Its frequency increases as the maternal age increases. Men with Klinefelter's Syndrome usually do not produce any sperm and are usually infertile, though there have been reports of men with Klinefelter's Syndrome who have become fathers.

This syndrome is treated by administering testosterone to the boys when they reach the age of puberty.

XYY (Super Male) Syndrome

Men with the XYY syndrome have been referred to as "super males." While the majority are very tall—over six feet—this is a misnomer, as many behave in a criminally aggressive manner. Because of their sociopathic behavior, many of them have difficulty at school and with authorities. Chromosome studies of inmates of prisons and mental institutions have identified many of these men. It seems that among patients with the XYY genic make-up there is an increased number of mentally retarded individuals. Reviews of cases with extra Y chromosomes have revealed the possibility of more congenital anomalies and more severe mental retardation as the number of Y chromosomes increases.

A popular defense technique of criminal attorneys is to plead innocence for their clients when they show an XYY chromosome abnormality. The alibi of the criminal is no longer "the devil made me do it," but "my chromosomes made me do it."

The Triple-X Females

Females with triple-X genic make-up can be normal physically and mentally, and can produce children. Daughters of these women are apt to have the same type of genic make-up and sons will have XXY, Klinefelter's Syndrome.

Children of women with amenorrhea, who have been medically treated for infertility, often are affected in this way. Women who are infertile should have a chromosome study before they are treated. Otherwise, they may produce offspring who have not only sexual underdevelopment, but also mental retardation.

Females who have four X chromosomes or more are very severely retarded.

Statistics show that there is approximately one triple-X female in every thousand live female births.

The X Chromosome

Murray Barr made an important discovery in the late 1940s (see McKusick). He found that in females the nuclei had a darkly staining chromatin mass along the nuclear membrane. This chromatin mass became known as the Barr body. It is found in all normal female tissue but not in normal male tissue. The Barr chromosome seems to be the resting X chromosome. It is believed that a cell cannot live without at least one X chromosome. Women with Turner's Syndrome do not have this chromatin mass, since they only have one X chromosome in their genic make-up. Males with

Klinefelter's Syndrome show a positive chromatin mass, which means that they have an extra X chromosome.

There is a long list of genic disorders that are attributed to the X chromosome. The wig industry thrives on one of these defects—the loss of scalp hair is believed to be sex-influenced. Since the male has only one X chromosome, if he has the gene for loss of hair of the scalp, he will manifest this disorder by losing his hair.

Other X-linked inherited disorders are Albinism, deafness syndrome, anus imperforation, cleft palate, with wide-set eyes and median frontal prominence of the skull, color blindness, deafness of the conductive type, hemophilia, Duchenne-type muscular dystrophy, congenital absence of teeth, and many others.

The Y-Linked Inheritance

The sex of the embryo is determined at the time of fertilization, but it is not until the seventh week of development that characteristics of either a male or a female appear. The Y chromosome is responsible for maleness.

Girls always are physically more mature than boys of the same age. The average girl's acceleration of growth comes earlier than the boy's growth development. This retardation of growth in boys is attributed to the Y chromosome.

It is believed that hairy ears (fig. 7.15) is a Y-linked inheritance. This trait is absent in females whose fathers have hairy ears. The same fathers produce sons with characteristically hairy ears.

Our sex is determined by our sex chromosomes. In this we see the importance of instant creation. The unfortunate individuals who have been classified as true hermaphrodites, having Turner's Syndrome or Klinefelter's Syndrome, show the evidence of the disaster that takes place when there are genic mistakes. How could maleness and femaleness evolve? This marvelous system had to have been instantly created. Any chromosomal abnormality causes disaster.

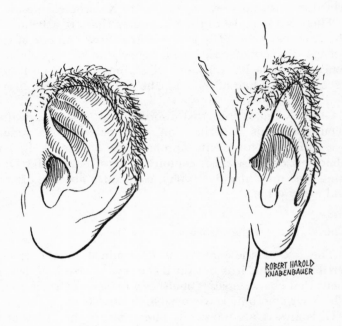

Fig. 7.15. Hairy ears, a Y-linked inheritance found only in males.

Why Disease?

Students who are interested in the origin of life eventually face the question: Why is there disease? If we had a loving Creator, why is there so much suffering in the world?

It is impossible to separate disease and suffering—the two go together. Disease is the absence of health, which may be caused by any alteration in the structure or functions of the body. Suffering can be caused by pain or grief.

Man's inhumanity to man can cause suffering and disease, as happened during the Nigerian Civil War. This caused a famine so that many children suffered and died from malnutrition and disease. The general who ordered his troops to fight and who seceded from the Nigerian nation, escaped unscathed to another country when he saw his cause was lost. Because mankind is so selfish and greedy, this type of war cannot be eliminated.

Infectious Disease

Sometimes we are innocent victims of contagious diseases, although immunizations have lessened the deadly effect of many of these diseases.

Sometimes the breaking of a moral law can cause disease. Illicit sex may result in venereal disease. Articles that call the attention of physicians to the prevention of venereal disease, fail to state that the keeping of the seventh commandment by young people would protect them from getting venereal diseases.

The breaking of the moral law can cause the speeding up of the law of decay and death. For example, a bank robber may be killed by a policeman's bullet when he attempts to rob a bank. It is obvious that the bank robber's body will undergo decay after death.

The breaking of certain health laws may result in disease and death. The health laws that Moses gave the Israelites are still good rules to follow today. The recent outbreak of cholera in Italy was due to the eating of contaminated shellfish. The ancient Hebrew health laws do not permit the eating of shellfish. By obeying the health laws, the outbreak of cholera could have been prevented.

Several years ago there was an outbreak of hepatitis along the eastern seaboard of the United States. It was soon noted by physicians that there was a conspicuous absence of Jewish patients among those having hepatitis. Public Health officials soon pointed to oysters as being the contaminated shellfish that caused the hepatitis.

In my opinion, infectious diseases are caused by organisms that have degenerated from their original creation. It was not the intention of the Creator to cause suffering and disease. How can this be proved? We know that the Creator did not create man as evil. It is man's rebellion that has caused suffering and disease. Both mankind and organisms have degenerated from their original state and purpose.

Parasitic Diseases

Parasites are organisms that live inside or upon man. One of the multicellular parasites that infest man is the little pinworm. It has been estimated that in the United States there are about 18 million persons infested with pinworms.

Degenerative Diseases

Degenerative diseases are due to the aging process. Normal wear and tear of the body will cause deterioration. Specific chemical causes may also be the reasons for some degenerative diseases.

Osteoarthritis

One of the most common degenerative diseases among elderly people is osteoarthritis. Patients complain of pain, which is relieved by rest. There is degeneration of the cartilage of the joint accompanied by an increase in the bone at the articular margins. Some of the more common causes of degenerative arthritis are overweight, bad posture, and occupational use of a joint (or joints). Many people who have typed for many years have this type of arthritis of their finger joints.

Arteriosclerosis

Arteriosclerosis is referred to as hardening of the arteries. There is a thickening of the muscle coats of the smallest arterioles because of an increase in blood pressure. Atherosclerosis is the most common form of arteriosclerosis. This type of sclerosis is associated with cholesterol, which is found in abundance in the walls of the arteries. Persons of all ages have been found to have some degree of atherosclerosis at autopsy. It is believed that the female hormones protect women to some degree from this degenerative disease. Before menopause, females have fewer deposits of cholesterol in walls of their arteries. After menopause, both sexes are equally affected. This type of sclerosis causes narrowing of the vessels, which can produce heart attacks and strokes.

Central Nervous System

Senile degeneration of the brain can take place independent of the cardiovascular system. These changes involve the nerve cells of the brain that undergo degeneration. Individuals undergo mental changes that are more involved than just memory loss.

It is obvious as age progresses that degenerative changes can take place in all the systems of the body. This shows that the process of decay and death is in effect.

The question arises again as to whether there was some type of super vitamin or vitamins in the fruit of the Tree of Life that would have prevented degenerative diseases.

8

The Age of the Earth, Moon, Stars, and Comets

How Old Is the Earth?

The age of the earth is closely associated with the history of the earth. We cannot study the one without making a study of the other. Moses gave a short, complete narrative of the creation of the earth and of the physical changes that resulted from man's disobedience. Some of these changes are discussed in "Decay and Death." Some of the most startling physical changes to the earth came from the Noachian Deluge. Let us examine some of the evidence of this great flood.

Water

Without an excessive amount of water, there could never have been a world-wide flood. Seventy-one percent of the earth's surface is covered with water, equal to 137 million square miles. It has been established that the water volume is eight times greater than the land mass projecting above the water of the seas and oceans.

Where did all this water come from? Moses clearly states that not only did it start to rain, but the fountains of the deep were broken up and burst forth causing the great flood. How did Moses know that there were great underground fountains or bodies of water? He did not know anything about oceanography or geology.

Prior to the fall of man, the Creator pronounced everything as being very good. Evidently the climate prior to the Flood was mild and pleasant. The great ice caps of the polar regions were evidently formed during a later period of time. The shift of the world's axis could have been a factor in the formation of these ice caps, as well as atmospheric evaporation of the water and then the transportation of this moisture to the polar regions, where it fell as snow. Oceanographers believe that if the polar caps were to melt today, most of the world's cities would be covered with water and only the highest mountain peaks would be visible.

There are mountain ranges and submerged canyons in the oceans. Where did they come from? Is it possible that some of these underwater mountains and canyons were formed during the reshaping of the earth's surface during and after the Flood period? It is possible that this is the period of time in which the continental drift took place. These canyons were formed by the great force of large amounts of water.

Prior to the Flood, the seas and the fountains of the deep existed. It is uncertain as to the amount of water that each contained.

Buried Vegetation

Buried vegetation is found throughout the earth. The end product of buried vegetation is coal. Deposits of coal are imbedded with sandstone and shale. Coal seams may be as much as 30 or 40 feet in thickness. In some the trunks of trees can be found in an upside-down position. Sometimes upright trees have been found in these coal seams. The evidence points to a catastrophic event that uprooted and buried this vegetation.

Successive petrified forests have been discovered in Yellowstone Park. It is believed that volcanic ash caused these trees to die and become petrified. The Petrified Forest of Arizona is probably the result of the Deluge.

Dinosaurs

Whatever happened to all the dinosaurs? The remains of
dinosaurs have been discovered in Canada's midwestern
plains, in Utah, and in Colorado. Many of these skeletal
specimens have been found and mounted and placed in
museums.

Dinosaurs varied in size and shape. Some were small, about
the size of a rabbit. The largest of the dinosaurs were at least
80 or more feet in length and could have weighed as much as
50 tons. Some of the dinosaurs were bipedal, walking on their
hind legs. Their forelimbs were proportionately shorter,
somewhat like those of the kangaroo. Another type of
dinosaur walked about on all four extremities. Fossil remains
of teeth, armor plates, and even skin have been found. Some
of these creatures were armed with horns, talons, or vicious-
looking teeth.

Many of these giant animals spent most of their lives living
in water. Their bones present a strange phenomenon which is
referred to as "waterline." Below the water line, the bones are
heavy and solid, whereas above the line they are lighter and
contain hollows. This ingenious structure permitted these
giant creatures to stay upright in the water.

Petrified fossil dinosaur eggs were found in the Gobi Desert
in Mongolia in 1923 and may be viewed at the American
Museum of Natural History. The unhatched embryo skeletons can be seen in the eggs.

Why did these giants disappear from the face of the earth?
Were they all struck down by disease at once? What caused
the dinosaurs that were capable of staying afloat to die? The
petrified fossil eggs show evidence of water being the cause of
their death and burial—a great catastrophe such as a flood.

Even to the evolutionists, the disappearance of the dinosaur is a problem. The fossil remains of dinosaurs have been
found throughout the world. Their disappearance cannot be
explained by local catastrophe. Some evolutionists believe
that the dinosaurs became extinct because of the failure of
the eggs to hatch, due to some biological phenomenon.

A universal catastrophic flood is a reasonable and acceptable explanation for the disappearance of the dinosaurs.

Fossil Sea Life

Geological literature points to the fact that fossil sea life is very prominent in the sedimentary rocks. It is difficult to imagine how this could be true. Why are plants, insects, reptiles, mammals, birds, extinct and modern fishes all found mixed up and piled together in a common fossil burial ground? Since birds are able to fly away from a storm or a flood, why are they buried with the sea life? Under ordinary environmental conditions sea life, plants, insects, mammals, etc., do not die together. The only explanation for their being buried together must be a catastrophic natural event, like a flood.

Frozen Mammoths

The frozen mammoths of Siberia and Alaska present a perplexing problem to those who adhere to the theory of uniformity. Evidently, these great herds of mammoths were grazing peacefully when they were suddenly overcome by freezing temperatures and froze to death. Many of these mammoths have been perfectly preserved for many centuries.

As previously mentioned, the sudden shifting of the earth's axis could have caused this sudden freezing in the polar regions of our earth. We know that the temperature must have been mild and sunny just before the deep freeze occurred. The animals were well fed. One had buttercups still in his mouth at the time he was frozen. Partially fossilized large trees have also been found in these northernmost areas where the mammoths grazed. In many places, the remains of ancient trees have been found in the frozen soil. These trees required a milder climate and no longer grow in these northernmost regions.

Mammoth ivory has been known for centuries to the Chinese, who have used the ivory for various articles and ornaments. Large deposits of mammoth bones and ivory are

found on the islands off Siberia. It is believed that even larger
deposits are under the sea surrounding these islands.

Fossil Graveyards

Many of the fossil graveyards have been found in sedimentary rocks, which have been laid down by moving water. As
mentioned previously, billions of fossil fish have been found
in sedimentary rocks. Many fossil remains are found grossly
out of place in the evolution time scale. Geological fossil
mixing was found in the cores taken from the depths of the
Pacific Ocean. Such mixing of fossils is referred to as
"displacement." Fossil graveyards are not occurring today.

Radioactive Clocks

The evolutionist points with pride to the radioactive clocks
as being a scientifically accurate way of dating rocks,
meteorites, and fossils. This is not completely true. They fail
to tell of the great assumptions that they make. Frequently,
these assumptions go unnoticed even by the evolutionists.

This is the way these mistaken assumptions come about.
For example, the evolutionists estimate a particular rock's
age to be 5 billion years. The age determination of the rock is
made by the ratio of uranium decay into lead. Because there
is enough lead in the rock to equal 5 billion years of time, this
is the estimated age of this particular rock. Here is the
mistaken assumption. The Creator could have made enough
lead in this particular rock to make it look either 2, 3, 4, or 5
billion years of age, or more. The evolutionist assumes that it
all started out as uranium.

Some scientists have voiced their disagreement with these
assumptions in geological literature. Such assumptions are
also made in carbon-14 and potassium-argon methods of
radioactive dating.

How much confidence would you have in a bank, in which
you deposited your hard-earned money, if they told you the
accuracy in their accounting department was only from 25 to

50 percent? You certainly would question their bookkeeping methods. Likewise, you should question the assumptions that are made in geological dating of the earth.

Professor Harold S. Slusher reviewed the use of radioactive clocks as a method of dating, in his book *Critique of Radioactive Dating*. Professor Slusher concluded that if Melvin A. Cook's Q-values are considered in doing the calculations, the supposed billions of years for the age of the earth by the evolutionists is reduced to a mere 8,000 to 10,000 years. (It is beyond the scope of this book to go into details concerning this problem. The Slusher reference in the bibliography gives more information on the Q-values and Professor Cook's work at the University of Utah.)

Historical Evidence

According to Bishop Ussher (see Whitcomb and Morris in the bibliography) the earth was created in 4004 B.C. From a biblical standpoint, the earth is approximately 6,000 years old.

Studies of the beginnings of ancient civilization correlate with the estimated age of 6,000 years of our earth. It is believed that the earliest Chinese culture began about 3400 B.C.; the earliest Egyptian civilization about 3110 B.C.; and the ancient Babylonian civilization about 3300 B.C. These three civilizations came upon the scene only after the Noachian Deluge.

The Jewish people have always kept their own calendar. According to their calendar, we are now in the year 5739.

The Noachian Deluge occurred about 1,600 years after the creation of the world. If we add this figure to the estimated beginning of these ancient civilizations, we come out with a historical estimate of the age of the earth.

It must be remembered that this is not a scientific estimate, only a historical estimate of the age of the earth.

The following question now arises: Is the estimated age of the earth by Bishop Ussher and the Jewish calendar more accurate and believable than the estimated age of the earth by radioactive dating? Remember the assumptions made in the calculations of radioactive dating methods using the Q-values.

The Earth's Age Measured by the Decay of Its Magnetic Field

Over 2,500 years ago the ancient Greeks experimented with the magnetism of rocks that could attract or repel iron. In 1269 a Frenchman by the name of Petrus de Maricourt performed an experiment with a small sphere of mineral magnetite. He placed bits of iron on the sphere, which concentrated at a point that he called the pole. It was generally believed that the strange forces that were able to move a compass came from the sky.

It was not until 1600 that an English physician, William Gilbert, recognized that the whole earth acted as a magnet. He first thought that the earth's core was a huge bar magnet connecting the North and South Poles, but an experiment changed his mind. He discovered that an iron bar magnet would lose its magnetic properties if it was heated to a red hot temperature. As soon as the iron bar cooled it regained its magnetism. He realized that the Earth's magnetism had to be due to some other factor because the very high temperatures inside of the earth would cause the iron bar to lose its magnetism.

In the early 1830s some English scientists became interested in the earth's magnetic field. Sir Horace Lamb conducted scientific experiments and then predicted the decay of the earth's magnetic field. This decay is not well publicized, because it is against the theory of an old age for the earth. It contradicts the possibility of the earth's being 3 to 5 billion years old.

In a paper published by Dr. Thomas G. Barnes, of the University of Texas at El Paso, it was stated that the earth's main magnetic field is decaying at a relatively rapid rate. The half-life is believed to be 1,400 years. The strength of the magnetic field is reduced by one-half every 1,400 years. The heat source from the core of the earth comes from radioactive decay of both long-lived and short-lived isotopes.

The earth's magnetic field is constantly shifting in position as well as decaying in strength. The changes in the magnetic field are due to the molten core.

If Dr. Barnes is correct in the estimate of the magnetic field's delay of one-half its strength every 1,400 years, it means that if we go back far enough in time, not only would the earth's core be molten, but the entire earth would be a liquid combustible mass like our sun. In other words, the earth could not have sustained life, as we know it, for more than 10,000 years. Thus, evolution and the tremendously long periods of time necessary for it are impossible.

The evolutionists never give up in their determination to justify the billions of years that life has supposedly existed on earth. Needing a theory to divert attention from the evidence presented by Dr. Barnes, the evolutionists proposed the dynamo theory of Professor Walter Elsasser of the Scripps Institute of Oceanography (see the Slusher reference in the bibliography). He postulated that the liquid motions within the core acted as a natural dynamo, which would generate electrical current, this producing a magnetic field. This theory does not explain the decay of the magnetic field.

It is believed that the heat of the earth's core is some of the heat that still remains from when the earth was first formed and that has been generated by the radioactivity within the earth's core.

The evidence of the decay of the earth's magnetic field points to a young earth. Instant creation of mass is the reverse of the destruction of mass by an atomic bomb. Thus we see that man can destroy matter, turning it into energy, but the Creator can create both mass and energy. If this seems difficult to understand, ponder Einstein's equation, energy equals mass times the acceleration of light to the second power.

Our Solar System

On a clear, cloudless night, the majesty of the Creator is revealed in the starry sky. The celestial stars are similar to our sun. The sun, which is a star, belongs to the Milky Way system, which is believed to have at least 100 billion suns. Our nearest celestial neighbor is Alpha Centauri, which is 4.28 light years from us. Another near neighbor of ours is Barnard's star, which is 5.98 light years from us. Barnard's star was studied by P. van de Kamp and his associates (see the Knox reference), who found that the motion of this star seemed to fluctuate periodically, due to an invisible companion planet. The planet which causes the Barnard's star to wiggle is estimated to be 1½ times the mass of Jupiter. There are other stars near us that also exhibit periodic fluctuations.

Planetary systems are quite common in the Universe. If one out of ten stars in our galaxy possesses a planetary system, then there are an enormous number of planetary systems. Who on earth can know the number of galaxies that exist? The enormous expanse of the universe staggers the imagination.

We are told in the Book of Job that the sons of the Creator shouted for joy at the creation of this solar system and the creation of man. These sons, the equivalent of Adam, live on other planets. They existed before the creation of our solar system.

There are many wonders and mysteries of our Creator's vast Universe. When studying astronomy one realizes that all is not by chance but is under law and great order. The majestic Creator of space meant it to be so. Dr. Erwin B. Frost, a former director of the Yerkes Observatory, stated: "There is no evidence that the Universe is automatic, or that it has within itself the power to make the laws which govern it. Mere matter cannot be endowed with this capacity. The Universe is not a haphazard aggregation of accidental bodies moving without system or order. It is the work of Omnipotence" (see Knox's *Wonder Worlds*). Also, Sir Isaac Newton believed this to be true when he stated that the existence of the Universe declares itself to be a miracle made by an infinite Power.

Comets

Comets, mysterious members of our solar system, are small in mass in comparison with other celestial bodies. But what they lack in size they make up for by their flamboyant appearance when they visit too near our earth's atmosphere.

The planets of our solar system revolve around the sun in orbits, which are nearly circular and approximately all in the same plane. The comets defy these rules. The comets' orbits are very eccentric and are inclined in various planes. They can be very elongated and take the comet deep into space, where it undergoes "cold storage." When the comet returns to the vicinity of the sun it begins to absorb heat from the sun, and the gas liberated from the comet forms the tail of the comet. Comets are divided into two types. The short-period comets appear every 50 years or less, whereas long-period comets' appearances are more than 50 years apart.

Where do comets come from? No one knows for sure. They may be the leftovers from the days of creation. A Dutch astronomer by the name of Oort postulated that the comets' cores came from asteroids which were ejected from their orbits (see Slusher's *Age of the Solar System*). Some have postulated that Jupiter has ejected comets from volcanoes. The reasons for these theories is the glaring evidence that comets are diminishing in number. Comets that we can see with the naked eye have become very scarce since 1900, because when comets come into contact with the sun and the planets they disintegrate. The "falling of the stars" on November 13, 1833 was due to the head of a comet passing through our earth's atmosphere. The writers of that day describe this spectacle as a shower of shooting stars, which were as numerous as snowflakes in a blizzard. Comets are relatively safe when they are at a far distance from the sun and are in cold storage because of their deepness into space, but as a comet leaves the cold storage area and approaches the sun it undergoes some disintegration. This disintegration is what occurred before the eyes of the people in 1833.

Professor Harold S. Slusher points out that since comets diminish in size and break up completely, no comet can exist for millions and even billions of years. This means that our solar system is much younger than the evolutionists' estimate of 3 to 5 billion years old.

The most famous comet of all is Halley's Comet. In 1682 Sir Edmund Halley, an astronomer, observed the comet at night, made some very careful calculations, and then predicted that the comet would reappear after 76 years. Halley was ridiculed and accused of looking for publicity. People reasoned that Halley knew that he would be dead before the comet would return. Halley's prediction of the return of the comet was right on schedule; it appeared on Christmas Eve, 1758. Halley's comet reappeared in 1835, in 1910, and it is due to visit us again in 1986.

Professor Slusher believes that our solar system is young because comets cannot exist for billions of years. Comets undergo disintegration. This means that the comets came into existence at the same time as the rest of our solar system.

The Moon's Surface

Before the moon's surface was explored, scientists were worried about a spaceship landing on the moon and then sinking down into a possibly enormous amount of dust on the moon's surface. The question arises as to what made the scientists think the dust on the moon's surface would be many feet deep? The reason is that astronomers thought the moon to be from 3 to 5 billion years old. Their assumption was incorrect.

Cosmic dust, which is present in space, reaches both the moon's and earth's surfaces. The average amount of dust that accumulates per year on the surface of the moon can be measured. When the total depth of the dust on the moon is divided by this figure, it reveals that the age of the moon is less than ten thousand years.

Why wasn't the public informed of this information? Our tax dollars paid for these space explorations. Did NASA suppress it because it contradicts the evolutionary theory? As taxpayers we have a right to all the facts, even when these facts do not support the theory of evolution.

9

Evolution or Instant Creation?

The General Pattern

There is a general pattern of design seen in both animal and plant life. The evolutionists interpret this as meaning that all creation came from a single source and progressed upward. In contrast, the anti-evolutionists believe that this similarity of design means a common Creator. Comparison studies of the anatomy of the vertebrates serve to illustrate this similarity of design.

Skin

There is a marvelous diversification in the skins of the various vertebrates. One of the simplest types of skin covering is found in marine life. The amphioxus, which gets its name from its spearlike appearance, is covered with a single epithelial layer. It lives among the sandy beaches throughout the world. The adults are from 1 to 3 inches long. In China it is gathered in sizable amounts and served as a gourmet's delight.

The skin of gnathostome fishes is more complex, as the epidermis consists of a thin layer of stratified squamous cells. This type also has dermal scales and unicellular glands.

There are higher groups of fishes that have an even more

complex skin. The reason some fishes feel so slippery is because of mucus, which comes from the unicellular mucous glands that rupture when they reach the outer surface of the skin. Fishes that do not have scales have an abundance of these mucous unicellular glands. Some fishes have poisonous glands at the base of the spines of their pectoral fins and may also have multicellular skin glands. Evolutionists claim that multicellular glands of certain fishes became modified to serve as light-emitting organs in deep-water fish. They state that the absence of light in the deep water caused the fish to develop the light-producing organ to permit them to see. We are told by the evolutionists that salamanders in dark caves have lost their sight. If this is so, why didn't the deep-water fishes lose their ability to see?

Instant creation is the only explanation for the ability of deep-water fishes to produce their own light. The loss of the ability to see by the salamanders shows degeneration. It is change, but it is not to a higher level.

The skin of amphibians becomes more specialized in order to meet their needs. Some toads have dermal scales, but for most amphibians scales are absent. The warty appearance of toads is caused by the thickening of the stratum corneum, the outermost layer of the epidermis. The skin of the amphibians has multicellular mucus-secreting glands.

The Creator gave the reptiles a skin that is unique. The stratum corneum is very thick. The epidermal scales and rattles are parts of the epidermis, which was designed by the Creator. Reptiles have a small number of skin glands, which results in a dry, scaly skin. This allows the reptiles to conserve water, which is necessary in the desert.

How do snakes find their mates? The secretions of the scent glands near the cloaca is involved in sexual attraction. As snakes slither along the trail they leave the secretion scent. This permits them to find each other in places where they hibernate.

Only by instant creation could such an elaborate system, such as the scent trail for sexual attraction, come into existence. The snakes needed the scent sexual attraction system in order to reproduce themselves. Can you imagine some poor snake waiting around millions of years trying to develop such a system?

Birds are referred to as being "thin-skinned." The skin is thicker on the head, feet, and legs. The legs of birds contain epidermal scales. The beak, claws, and feathers of birds are said to be epidermal modifications of skin by evolution (see the section on birds).

The skin of mammals is even more complex. The skin appendages, claw, nail, and hoof are designed for the particular needs of the animal (see the section on the skin).

The pigmentation of the epidermis of vertebrates can serve as a protective mechanism. The reflection and absorption of light by cells that contain pigment granules produce the various color patterns seen in the skins of fishes, amphibians, and reptiles. The pigment granules in the cell are found either around the nucleus or dispersed throughout the cytoplasm of the cell. The location of pigment granules is under the control of the sympathetic nervous system and of hormones. The dispersion of the granules is caused by a hormone produced in the intermediate lobe of the pituitary gland. It will cause darkening of the skin. The blanching of the skin, which is caused by the collection of the granules around the nucleus, is the result of a hormone produced by the pineal body. Brown, yellow, and red granules produce the different colors. Another type of granule produces a rainbowlike color effect.

The ability of some creatures to disguise themselves serves as a means of protection. Have you ever watched a lizard change colors? A lizard will take on the colorations of its surroundings. Just about everyone has prodded lizards from one resting spot to another area to watch them change color. On a brown area a lizard will look brown. When the lizard is forced to an area where there is a green coloration, it will take on a green coloration disguise. Who made the lizard a master at camouflage? How could such a system evolve when it's under such regulation and control? The system is obviously a preplanned protective mechanism.

Skeletal System

The skulls of vertebrates increase in complexity, designed in by the Creator, to suit the needs of the organism. There are many variations in skull types. In the mammal there is a definite decrease in the number of skull bones in comparison to the reptilian type.

Snakes have their own uniqueness. Most snakes lack limb girdles and a sternum. So-called vestiges of the pelvis and the hind limbs are found in the boas and pythons. It would be an interesting experiment to remove these vestiges and see how well the snakes got along so far as locomotion is concerned. The so-called phylogenetic origin of the sternum is somewhat obscure. In the embryos of amphibians and mammals the sternum develops from connective tissue that is independent of the ribs. The sternum arises from two ventral collagenous bars in the reptiles and birds. Only those vertebrates that walk have sternums.

The Creator used a basic pattern for the appendicular (extremities) skeleton. The anterior limbs or wings of birds are well designed for flight. There is a reduction in the number of carpal bones and digits of their wings. The bones are designed with pneumatic channels that reduce their weight. The muscles provide the power for flight. The feathers provide the appropriate "wingspan" to get airborne and to maintain flight.

The bat's basic plan is unique. It uses its webbed forelimbs to catch insects while it is in flight.

The similarity of the basic plans for the extremities can be seen in the skeletons. Does this mean that they all had a common origin or a common Creator?

Frequently artists and musicians have certain characteristic features in their work that distinguish them from others. This is exactly what the basic pattern of the skeletal system shows. We all share a common Creator.

Margins of Safety

Medical students learn early in their training that the body has many built-in margins of safety within its various structural and functional systems. How great is the depth and knowledge and wisdom of the Creator: These measures of safety were designed for our protection.

Our very survival depends on some of these safety measures, which a thoughtful Creator provided. Some have been mentioned previously.

Suppose that someone gains twice as much weight as he should have for his particular height and build. His bones and muscles will still be able to take care of the extra load. Obesity can cause problems of the cardiovascular system, joints, etc., but the point is the body can make adjustments for the extra weight and the muscular and skeletal systems will adjust to it.

The respiratory system also has its safeguards. The coughing reflex warns us that tobacco smoke is not acceptable to the respiratory system. Suppose that a person develops cancer of the lung and has surgery. Has he used up all his margins of safety? He may survive with one lung if he does not have emphysema. It is possible for one lung to remain collapsed from birth, as people can survive on one normal lung.

The kidneys also have a margin of safety. A baby born with one kidney can have a normal life span.

The body has limits beyond which it is not safe to go. Chronic fatigue can result in individuals who hold down two jobs. They frequently pay an extraordinary price for their overwork.

Pain can also be a signal that we are overstepping a margin of safety. A tight shoe can cause pain and discomfort before a blister develops. Appropriate measures should be taken when we receive a painful warning.

The Creator has provided most of us with enough common

sense to have good judgment. In my opinion, taking illicit drugs, riding motorcycles, and hang gliding are overstepping the bounds of safety that good judgment indicates.

Car safety has been an issue in the country for several years now. Federal laws had to be passed to get safety devices added to American cars. Normal persons are born with their margins of safety. How could they ever have evolved? They may not ever be used except when needed, as in an emergency such as when pain or hemorrhage occurs.

Genetic Variations

This discussion will deal primarily with normal variations within a population, which occur within rather narrow limits. For example, five daughters of the same parents vary in height from 5 to 6 feet tall. Their grandmothers were extremely short women. This variation is normal.

The degree of pigmentation of children from the same parents can vary greatly. One child can be of the Scandinavian type, tall and blond. Another child in the same family can be of the Mediterranean type, with an olive complexion and dark eyes. These children have ancestors who are of Scandinavian and of Latin descent.

I know of a man who always suspected that he was illegitimate because he did not look like his brothers and sisters. Late in life his brothers and sisters developed an inherited metabolic disease. He was convinced more than ever that he was illegitimate. He presented the hereditary differences to his mother when he was 45 years of age. She then told him that he had a different father from his brothers and sisters. This man did not share the abnormal variation that his brothers and sisters had. Having a different father evidently kept him from developing this particular disease.

From ancient times, man has been interested in breeding fast race horses. Any horse that wins many races is eventually used for stud services. Horse breeders know that fast racing horses will have offspring who are apt to be fast race horses. There is still a limit on how fast even the fastest horse can run, since genetics limits this.

Poultrymen have always been interested in having hens lay the maximum number of eggs per year. There is no hen alive that can lay 5 eggs a day 365 days a year. There is a physiological limit to the number of eggs a hen can lay per year.

The color of moths is related to survival. Dark-colored moths have a better survival rate in the industrial regions of England. It is normal for moths to rest upon trunks of trees during periods of inactivity. Many of the trees in that area are blackened because of coal particles. The dark-colored moths are less visible on the blackened trunks. The whitish colored moths do not fare so well because birds are able to see them so much more easily. Variations in the pigmentation of moths determine their natural selection.

In the unpolluted countryside the black moths are picked off the tree trunks by the birds. The tree trunks in the countryside are free of coal particles and are grayish in color. Therefore, the dark-colored moths are more easily seen by the birds.

The survival rate of the moth is determined by its color as well as by the color of the tree trunks. According to evolution, insects evolved before birds. How could the moth's evolvement take this into account if there were no birds around? Isn't it more logical that the Creator put this variation ability within the genetic system of the moth?

It must be remembered that the moth is still a moth and it has not evolved into something else. Natural selection and variation are determining factors in the moth's survival, but these factors will not change the moth into some other creature.

Mutations

Even the evolutionists have to admit that there is overwhelming evidence that mutations have a deleterious effect. They insist, however, that gradual, slow variations cause evolution. This cannot be demonstrated. All changes that take place must involve the DNA. (See the chapters on the Missing Links and From Molecules to Man.)

Frequently an evolutionist will refer to a bacteria's ability to resist a drug as a mutation. It is true that a bacteria may become resistant to penicillin, for example, the bacteria gonococcus. But the gonococcus does not evolve into something else. Evidently the bacteria has some type of immune system which causes it to have resistance to the penicillin.

Adaptation

Adaptation is the ability of a plant or an animal to adjust to the conditions of the environment so that it may exist. In order for the organism to exist, there must be a suitable environment. The environmental conditions must suit the physiological needs of the organism. The fish must have water and food to sustain life. There are some sea mammals that do come out of the water for periods of time. But how long would a seal exist on the desert without water? Not very long, because he is out of his normal environment.

There must be enough harmony between the organism and its environment so that the organism may live and reproduce itself.

The evolutionists tell us that the dinosaurs were unable to compete with some of the newly evolved creatures. Another theory suggests that these reptiles were wiped out because of their inability to adjust to the very cold climate. But in the fossil record, the evidence points to other reasons. Fossilized dinosaur eggs have been found with young embryos, which appear to be developing normally. What conditions caused these eggs to be fossilized? What conditions brought about the death of these dinosaurs, which are found in fossil beds in Utah and Colorado in the National Dinosaur Monument?

A change in environment can cause death. The Creator designed organisms to fit their environment. This is why evolution of lower forms of life to higher forms of life is impossible. All systems must be suitable to the environment.

I recall being told that whales were land animals that

decided to return to the sea. Their legs eventually developed into fins. This question arises: Since they returned to a water environment, why didn't their lungs revert back into gills? Isn't it reasonable to believe that the whale is in a state of perfect creation because it is suited perfectly to its environment?

Penguins are flightless birds, which spend the greater part of their lives in water. They are capable of swimming 25 miles per hour by diving and surfacing repeatedly. In the cold Antarctica, they slide on their bellies on the snow, using their flippers and feet to propel them. They can also assume the upright position for walking on shore.

The penguins are an ingeniously designed creation. They are capable of adapting to the frigid climate of the Antarctica as well as to the warmer climate of the Galapagos Islands near the Equator.

The evolutionists believe that birds evolved from reptiles. They say feathers developed from modified scales for the purpose of flight. Would the evolutionist have us believe that penguins were evolving feathers for the purpose of flight? Sea gulls are capable of flying and also fishing for their food. Why is one capable of flying and the other not?

The Creator foresaw the absurdity of the theory of evolution. The creation of the penguins is one of the many monkey wrenches that the Creator has thrown into the theory of evolution.

Do you know of any organism whose design could be improved upon to fit its natural environment? Isn't the honeybee well designed for the service that it performs? The only exception to this is the human race, and it is our heritage of evil which causes the conflict in the world and with our environment.

The Recapitulation Theory

During the last century, several individuals advocated the Recapitulation Theory, which is also known as the Biogenetic Law (see Storer, *General Zoology*).

A German scientist, Karl von Baer, contributed to this new biological concept. In 1828, he published his findings concerning embryonic development. These findings became known as Baer's Law, which states: (1) General characters appear before special characters. (2) From the more general the less general and finally the special characters develop. (3) An animal during development departs progressively from the form of other animals. (4) The young stages of an animal are like the young (or embryonic) stages of other animals lower in the scale but not like the adults of those animals.

These statements are not entirely true. In embryonic life, man never has true gill slits or a tail.

In 1864, Fritz Muller gave his own interpretation to Baer's Law. He taught that higher forms of life repeated their origin from lower forms of life during their embryonic development and that they also added new stages to their embryonic development because of their higher adult life requirements.

In 1868, Ernst Haeckel formulated the fraud of the Recapitulation Theory, "Biogenetic Law" (see McCann *God or Gorilla?*). He postulated that the development of an individual during its embryonic life (ontogeny) recapitulates the stages through which its ancestors passed (phylogeny).

Ernst Haeckel published a series showing the similarities of vertebrate embryos during their successive and comparable stages of development. (See figure 9.1, Haeckel's illustration of the embryos, and compare it with the normal human embryo, figure 2.9). In 1906, this fraud by Haeckel was brought to the public's attention in Germany. Professor Arnold Brass charged Haeckel with deliberate falsification of the illustration of the embryos. The evolutionists, who still write the textbooks for the students, do not point this out.

Most students are deeply impressed by multisyllable words such as recapitulation, ontogeny, and phylogeny. Students also believe that there is great scientific significance to anything that is called a law, such as Baer's Law and the Biogenetic Law. The reader should review the chapter that presents evidence against recapitulation. This chapter discusses the baby born with a tail, the coccyx, and other vestiges.

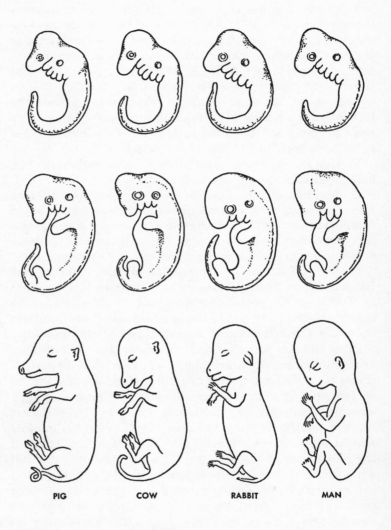

Fig. 9.1. Mammal embryos by Haeckel. Compare man embryos of Haeckel with normal human embryos and fetuses in chapter on Human Tails. The heads of Haeckel's man embryos are not correct. They have been altered to look like the animal embryos.

There are other developmental factors that disprove the theory of recapitulation. The fact that embryos may have similar features during their development does not mean that we all come from a common ancestor. It does mean that all forms of life did have the same Creator. Both Chevy and Cadillac cars are made by General Motors. They have features in common and their shape and design are similar. But a Chevy has never evolved into a Cadillac.

Others have realized the falseness of the doctrine of the Recapitulation Theory. William Ballard states: "No false biological statement has had a longer or more popular life than the one about the ontogeny of the four-chambered mammalian heart recapitulating its phylogeny from the two-chambered fish heart and the three-chambered amphibian or reptilian heart. Often repeated in the days when Haeckel's so-called biogenetic laws were widely and uncritically accepted, it can still be found in some elementary texts, side-by-side with correctly labelled diagrams of the two-chambered fish heart and the three-chambered frog heart."

Similarities between embryos and adult forms are not the result of common origins. Instead, similar patterns of development of embryos and adult forms of life are the result of a common Creator for all.

Instant Creation—Not Evolution

Our solar system and all created life were completed by the Creator's hand in a very short period of time. This is instant creation when compared to the four or five billion years that the evolutionists claim that it took creation to reach its present form. The unlimited power or energy of the Creator is used to transform energy into mass. This is not in contradiction to Einstein's theory—with the atomic bomb mass can be transformed into energy.

Even though it takes time to make an atom bomb, the destruction that it causes when set off is instantaneous. Mass is being transformed into energy. Instant creation by the

Creator is the opposite of the atom bomb (matter into energy). Energy is transformed by the Creator into mass.

Darwin and other evolutionists of his time did not know anything about enzyme activity. Cellular activity is under enzyme control. Enzyme activity controls our growth and development from the time of conception until death. All of the body's systems function because of enzymes.

How much work can an enzyme molecule do? Lehninger has estimated that a single enzyme molecule is capable of carrying out as many as several million catalytic cycles in one minute. This contradicts the evolution theory that change took place by a slow process. The absence of an enzyme can cause disease and death.

As students we are told that science is truth. The law of gravity is a scientific law; we know it to be true. Therefore, when students are told there is scientific evidence that proves the theory of evolution, they accept this as being true. Unless a student has a very critical mind, he accepts the interpretation of the facts as his teacher or science book tells him.

For example, the student is told that a small skull pictured in his textbook is one of his apelike ancestors. This is one viewpoint. But the real diagnosis is a microcephalic skull of a mentally retarded human being. From my own observation, many teachers in schools and universities are uninformed about different viewpoints.

After a person becomes more knowledgeable about different ways of looking at the so-called evidence, evolution will no longer be a sacred cow. Instead, evolution will turn out to be a lot of monkeyshine.

From a scientific viewpoint, the evolution of man from lower forms of life is impossible. Decay and death will eventually catch up with all living systems.

Glossary

Amphioxus - a member of a class of acranial chordates.

Anomaly - noticeable deviation from normal standards.

ATP - adenosine triphosphate.

Avitaminosis - deficiency disease caused by a deficiency of one or more vitamins.

A-V node - atrioventricular node; small mass of tissue lying in the wall of the right auricle, passing impulses received from the sinoatrial node by way of the atrioventricular bundles.

Caudal - posterior; relating to any anatomical structure resembling a tail.

Cholecystokinin - a hormone liberated by the upper intestinal mucosa on contact with gastric contents.

Coacervate - piled up; growing in dense clusters.

Coccyx - last bone at the lowermost end of the spine.

Collagen - protein responsible for most support in connective tissues; normal fibular connective tissue found in true skin.

Congenital defect - malformation or disorder present at birth.

Cyanosis - dark bluish or purplish coloration of the skin indicating deficient oxygenation of the blood.

Dermal sinus - a channel extending from the skin to a deeper lying structure, most frequently the spinal cord.

Distal - farthest from the center of the body; farthest from the trunk (referring to segments of the extremities).

DNA - deoxyribonucleic acid; the determinant of cell development.

Ductus arteriosus - a fetal vessel connecting the left pulmonary artery with the descending aorta, whose failure to close postnatally causes a cardiovascular handicap that can be dealt with surgically.

Duodenum - first division of the small intestine (about twelve finger-breadths in length) extending from the opening of the pylorus to the jejunum near the second lumbar vertebra.

Edema - swelling; abnormal perceptible accumulation of fluid in body tissues.

Epidermis - outer layer of skin.

Etiology - study of the cause of a disease, or the reasons for a disease as determined by medical diagnosis.

Fistula - abnormal tubelike passage leading from one abcess cavity or hollow organ to another or to the skin.

Follicle - a small cavity or depression; a small lymph node.

Glomerulus - small, rounded mass of capillary loops serving as filtering structures in the formation of urine in the kidney.

Gluteus maximus - the outermost of three muscles found in each of the human buttocks.

Hemangioma - birthmark involving overgrowth of small blood vessels in the skin.

Herniated - relating to any structure protruded through a hernia opening.

Hypoglycemia - an abnormally small concentration of glucose in the circulating blood.

Hypotension - subnormal arterial blood pressure.

Lanugo hair - fine, soft hair with minute shafts and large papillae, occurring on forehead, ears, and flanks.

Lipoma - fatty tumor.

Lordosis - sway back, caused by an increase in the forward curvature of the lower spine.

Lumbosacral - relating to the lumbar spine (section between the ribs and the pelvis) and the sacrum (broad, slightly curved, spade-shaped bone closing in the pelvic girdle at the back).

Lumen - space in the interior of a tubular structure, such as an artery or intestine.

Lymphoid - resembling lymph or lymphatic tissue.

Macrocephaly - having a long, large head.

Megacephaly - having a large head, either congenital or acquired.

Melanin - dark brown, black, or almost black pigment, normally occurring in the skin, hair, pigmental coat of the retina, and inconstantly in the medulla and the zona reticularis of the adrenal gland.

Microcephaly - abnormal smallness of the head.

Micrognathia - smallness of the jaws, especially the under jaw.

Mitochondria - granules and filaments existing in the cytoplasm and forming an essential part thereof.

Mongolism - a form of congenital idiocy characterized by a very low mentality and by abnormal body characteristics, including slanting eyes and a small, round head, flat in the back.

Neural groove - longitudinal hollow separating the neural crest from the main body of the neural plate.

Phalanx, -ges - the long bones of the fingers and toes.

Phosphorylation - the addition of phosphate to an organic compound.

Polydactylism - the presence of more than five digits on either hands or feet.

Prognathism - an abnormal projection forward of one or both jaws.

Purkinje system - network of intracardial conducting tissue made up of syncytial Purkinje fibers that lie in the myocardium and constitute the atrioventricular bundle and other conducting tracts which spread out from the sinus node.

Pyruvic acid - colorless liquid derived from distillation of tartaric acid, an intermediate compound in the metabolism of carbohydrates; in thiamine deficiency its oxidation is retarded and it accumulates in the tissues, especially in nervous structures.

Renal - of, relating to, or involving the kidneys.

Ribosome - a small structure in the cytoplasm of cells that carries on protein synthesis.

RNA - ribonucleic acid.

S-A node - a small mass of tissue made up of Purkinje fibers, ganglion cells, and nerve fibers, embedded in the musculature of the right auricle of higher vertebrates, serving as a pacemaker to the heart.

Scoliosis - lateral curvature of the spine.

Sebaceous - relating to, secreting, or composed of fatty matter.

Somite - one of the paired, metamerically arranged cell masses formed in the dorsal or segmental zone of the mesoderm (middle skin layer).

Sphincter - an orbicular muscle which serves, when in a state of normal contraction, to close one of the orifices of the body.

Sternocleidomastoidus - muscle relating to the sternum, clavicle, and mastoid process.

Stratigraphy - sectional photography by X-rays.

Tachycardia - rapid beating of the heart.
Thyroglossal - relating to the thyroid and the tongue.
Thymectomy - operative removal of the thymus gland.

Vasoconstriction - narrowing of the blood vessels.

Bibliography

Abramoff, Peter. *Biology of Immune Response*. New York: McGraw-Hill Book Company, 1970.

Anderson, M. H., Bechtol, C. O., and Sollars, R. E. *Clinical Prosthetics for Physicians and Therapists*. Springfield, Il.: Charles C. Thomas Publishers, 1959.

Anderson, W. A. D., editor. *Pathology*, Vol. 1. Fifth Edition. St. Louis: C. V. Mosby Company, 1966.

Arey, Leslie Bainerd. *Developmental Anatomy*. Philadelphia: W. B. Saunders Company, 1965.

Balinsky, B. I. *An Introduction to Embryology*. Philadelphia: W. B. Saunders Company, 1965.

Ballard, William W. *Comparative Anatomy and Embryology*. New York: The Ronald Press, 1964.

Barnes, Thomas G. "Electromagnetics of the Earth's Field and Evaluation of Electric Conductivity, Current, and Joule Heating in the Earth's Core." *Creation Research Society Quarterly,* Vol. 9, March 1973.

Barrett, James T. *Textbook of Immunology*. St. Louis: C. V. Mosby Company, 1970.

Bascom, Willard. *A Hole in the Bottom of the Sea*. Garden City, N.Y.: Doubleday & Company, 1961.

Bateson, William. *Materials for the Study of Variation Discontinuity*. New York: The Macmillan Company, 1894.

Beeson, Paul D., and McDermott, Walsh. *Cecil-Loeb Text-*

book of Medicine. Philadelphia: W. B. Saunders Company, 1963.

Berry, William B. N. *Growth of a Prehistoric Time Scale.* San Francisco: W. H. Freeman & Company, 1968.

Bowers, Dorrance. "Marfan's Syndrome and the Weill-Marchesani Syndrome in the S. Family." *Annals of Internal Medicine,* Vol. 51, 1959.

Boyd, William. *Textbook of Pathology.* Eighth Edition. Philadelphia: Lea & Febiger, 1970.

Branch, C. H. Hardin. *Aspects of Anxiety.* Philadelphia: J. B. Lippincott, 1965.

Centerwall, Willard R. "Phenylketonuria." *Journal of the American Medical Association,* Vol. 165, September 28, 1957.

Chusid, Joseph G., and McDonald, Joseph J. *Correlative Neuroanatomy and Functional Neurology.* Los Altos, Calif.: Lange Medical Publications, 1958.

Clark, Harold W. *Fossils, Food, and Fire.* Escondido, Calif.: Outdoor Pictures, 1968.

Coffin, Harold G. *Creation—Accident or Design?* Washington, D.C.: Review and Herald Publishing Association, 1969.

Colbert, Edwin H. *Dinosaurs, Their Discovery and Their World.* New York: E. P. Dutton & Company, 1962.

Dallaire, L., and Fraser, F. C. "Two Unusual Cases of Familial Mongolism." *Canadian Journal of Genetics and Cytology,* Vol. 4, 1964.

Darwin, Charles. *The Origin of the Species by Means of Natural Selection.* Chicago: William Benton Publishers, Encyclopaedia Brittanica, 1952.

Davson, Hugh; Eggleton, M. Grace; and Starling, Evans. *Principles of Human Physiology.* Edited by Lovatt Evans. Fourteenth edition. Philadelphia: Lea & Febiger, 1968.

deCamp, L. Sprague. *The Great Monkey Trail.* Garden City, N.Y.: Doubleday & Company, 1968.

de Laubenfels, M. W. *Life Science.* New York: Prentice-Hall, 1949.

de Wardener, H. E. *The Kidney.* Third edition. Boston: Little, Brown & Company, 1967.

Dietrich, John H. *The Fathers of Evolution.* Minneapolis: The First Unitarian Society, 1927.

Dixon, Malcolm, and Webb, Edin C. *Enzymes.* New York: Academic Press, 1964.

Dodson, Edward O. *Evolution: Process and Product.* New York: Reinhold Publishing Corporation, 1960.

Dodson, R. S. *Dr. Clyde Fisher's Exploring the Heavens.* New York: Thomas Y. Crowell, 1964.

Duchenne, G. B. *Physiology of Motion.* Philadelphia: W. B. Saunders Company, 1959.

Eaton, Murray. "The Inadequacies of Neo-Darwinian Evolution as a Scientific Theory." *Mathematical Challenges to the Neo-Darwinian Interpretation of Evolution.* Edited by Paul S. Moorhead and Martin M. Kaplan. Philadelphia: Wister Institute Press, 1967.

Encyclopaedia Britannica, Vol. 17, p. 552. Chicago and London: Encyclopaedia Britannica, Inc., 1973.

Encyclopedia Americana. Vol. 3, p. 9; vol. 4, p. 646; vol. 6, p. 496; vol. 8, p. 481; vol. 10, p. 21; vol. 17, p. 879; and vol. 24, p. 425. New York: Americana Corporation, 1961.

Evans, Loren H.; Jenny, Jacques; and Roker, Charles W. "Surgical Correction of Polydactylism in the Horse." *Journal of the American Veterinary Association.* 146: 1405, June, 1965.

Finerty, John C., and Cowdry, E. V. *A Textbook of Histology.* Philadelphia: Lea & Febiger, 1962.

Frasier, F. Clarke, and McKusick, Victor A., Editors. *Congenital Malformations.* Amsterdam, N.Y.: Excerpta Medica, 1970.

Fuller, Robert W.; Brownlee, Raymond B.; and Baker, D. Lee. *Elements of Physics.* Boston: Allyn & Bacon, 1952, p. 51.

Gellis, Sidney S., and Feingold, Murray. *Atlas of Mental Retardation Syndromes.* Washington, D.C.: U.S. Department of Health, Education, and Welfare, 1968.

Goodman, Richard M., ed. *Genetic Disorders of Man.* First Edition. Boston: Little, Brown & Company, 1970.

————. "Huntington's Chorea." *Archives of Neurology.* Vol. 15, October 1966, pp. 345-55.

Gordon, Benjamin Lee, and Fork, Denys K. *Essentials of Immunology.* Philadelphia: F. A. Davis Company, 1971, pp. 6, 70.

Gray, Henry. *Anatomy of the Human Body.* Edited by Warren H. Lewis. Twenty-fourth edition. Philadelphia: Lea & Febiger, 1942, pp. 104, 105, 420, 442, 470.

Green, David E., and Goldberger, Robert F. *Molecular Insights into Living Processes.* New York: Academic Press, 1967, p. 407.

Gregory, William H., and Goldman, Edward H. *Biological Science for High School.* New York: Ginn & Company, 1965.

Gross, Jerome. "Collagen." *Scientific American,* May 1961, pp. 121-130.

Gunther, Albert C. L. C. *An Introduction to the Study of Fishes.* New York: Hafner Publishing Company, 1963.

Guyton, Arthur C. *Functions of the Human Body.* Third Edition. Philadelphia: W. B. Saunders Company, 1969.

Hall, Charles A. *The Blood in Disease.* Philadelphia: J. B. Lippincott, 1968.

Hansotia, P.; Cleeland, C. S.; and Chun, R. W. M. "Juvenile Huntington's Chorea." *Neurology,* Vol. 18, March 1968.

Hardin, Garrett. *Nature and Man's Fate.* New York: Mentor Books, 1961.

Harper, Harold A. *Review of Physiological Chemistry.* Los Altos, Calif.: Lange Medical Publications, 1969.

Hoerfein, B. F. *Canine Neurology.* Philadelphia: W. B. Saunders Company, 1965.

Hoffing, Charles K. *Textbook of Psychiatry for Medical Practice.* Second edition. Philadelphia: J. B. Lippincott, 1968.

Howorth, Henry H. *The Mammoth and the Flood.* London: Sampson Low, 1887.

Hull, D. E. "Thermodynamics and Kinetics of Spontaneous Generation." *Nature,* May 28, 1960, Vol. 186, p. 694.

Introduction to Medicine: Hematology Section Syllabus. Loma Linda University School of Medicine, 1972-73, pp. 93-96.

Jacobs, J. A. *The Earth's Core and Geomagnetism.* New York: The Macmillan Company, 1963.

Job 38:4-7.

Johnson, Willis H.; Laubengayer, Richard A.; Delanney, Louis E.; and Cole, Thomas A. *Biology.* Third edition. New York: Holt, Rinehart & Winston, 1966.

Kempe, C. Henry; Silver, Henry K.; and O'Brien, Donough. *Current Pediatric Diagnosis and Treatment.* Los Altos, Calif.: Lange Medical Publications, 1972.

Kent, George C. *Comparative Anatomy of the Vertebrates.* Second edition. St. Louis: C. V. Mosby Company, 1969.

Kleiner, Israel, and Orten, James M. *Biochemistry.* Seventh edition. St. Louis: C. V. Mosby Company, 1966.

Knox, Phillip L. *Wonder Worlds.* Los Angeles: The Voice of Prophecy, 1964.

Kopal, Zdenek. *The Solar System.* London: Oxford University Press, 1973.

Krupp, Marcus A.; Chatton, Milton J.; and Margen, Sheldon. *Current Diagnosis and Treatment.* Los Altos, Calif.: Lange Medical Publications, 1971.

Krusen, Frank H., Editor. *Handbook of Physical Medicine and Rehabilitation.* Philadelphia: W. B. Saunders Company, 1965.

Lagler, Karl F.; Bardach, John E.; and Miller, Robert R. *Ichthyology.* Ann Arbor: The University of Michigan Press, 1962.

Langman, Jan. *Medical Embryology.* Second edition. Baltimore: Williams and Wilkins, 1969.

Last, R. J. *Aids to Anatomy.* Twelfth edition. London: Bailliere, Tindall, & Cox, 1962.

Lehninger, Albert L. *Bioenergetics.* Second edition. Menlo Park, Calif.: W. A. Benjamin, 1971.

Long, E. John. *New Worlds of Oceanography.* New York: Pyramid Publications, 1965.

Lyman, Frank P. *Phenylketonuria.* Springfield, Ill.: Charles C. Thomas, 1963.

MacBeth, Norman. *Darwin Retired—An Appeal to Reason.* Boston: Bambit, Inc., 1971.

McCann, Alfred Watterson. *God or Gorilla?* New York: Devin-Adair Company, 1922.

McKusick, V. A. *Human Genetics.* Englewood Cliffs, N.J.: Prentice-Hall, 1969.

McKusick, V. A., and Rimoin, D. L. "General Tom Thumb and Other Midgets." *Scientific American,* Vol. 217, 1967.

Marples, Mary J. *The Ecology of the Human Skin.* Springfield, Ill.: Charles C. Thomas Publisher, 1965.

Marshall, A. J. *Biology and Comparative Physiology of Birds.* New York: Academic Press, 1960.

Meschan, Isadore. *Roentgen Signs in Practice.* Vol. 1. Philadelphia: W. B. Saunders Company, 1966, pp. 464-466.

Montagna, William. Comparative Anatomy. New York: John Wiley & Sons, 1959.

———. *The Structure and Function of Skin.* Second edition. New York: Academic Press, 1962.

Moody, Paul Amos. *Introduction to Evolution.* Second edition. New York: Harper & Brothers, 1962.

Morris, Henry. *Scientific Creationism.* San Diego: Creation Life Publishers, 1974.

Morris, Henry M. *Evolution: Thermodynamics and Entropy No. 3.* San Diego: Institute for Creation Research, 1971.

More, Louis T. *The Dogma of Evolution.* Princeton, N.J.: Princeton University Press, 1925.

Nason, Alvin, and Goldstein, Philip. *Biology 4, Introduction to Life.* Menlo Park, Calif.: Addison-Wesley Publishing Company, 1969.

Nelson, Waldo E. *Textbook of Pediatrics.* Eighth edition. Philadelphia: W. B. Saunders Company, 1964.

Otto, James H., and Towle, Albert. *Modern Biology.* New York: Holt, Rinehart & Winston, 1969.

Patten, Bradley M. *Human Embryology.* Second edition. Baltimore: Williams & Watkins Company, 1969.

Penrose, L. S., and Smith, G. F. *Down's Anomaly.* Boston: Little, Brown, 1966.

Perry, Thomas Martin, and Miller, Frank Nelson. *Pathology—A Dynamic Introduction to Medicine and Surgery.* Second edition. Boston: Little, Brown, 1971.

Post, Joseph, and Hoffman, Joseph. "Cell Renewal Patterns." *New England Journal of Medicine.* Vol. 279, August 1, 1968.

Potter, Edith L. *Pathology of Fetus and Newborn.* Second edition. Chicago: Year Book Medical Publishers, 1961.

Ranson, Stephen Walter. *The Anatomy of the Nervous System.* Seventh edition. Philadelphia: W. B. Saunders Company, 1943.

Ritland, Richard M. *A Search for Meaning in Nature.* Mountain View, Calif.: Pacific Press Publishing Association, 1970.

Rushmer, Robert F. *Cardiovascular Dynamics.* Third edition. Philadelphia: W. B. Saunders Company, 1970.

Sarkar, S. S.; Banerjee, A. R.; Bhattacharjee, Papia; and Stern, Curt. "A Contribution to the Genetics of Hypertrichosis of the Ear Rims." *American Journal of Human Genetics.* Vol. 12, 1961.

Simpson, George Gaylord. *Tempo and Mode in Evolution.* Morningside Heights, N.Y.: Columbia University Press, 1947.

Slusher, Harold S. "Age of the Solar System." Parts I and II. *Acts and Facts of Institute for Creation Research,* July and August, 1973.

————. *Critique of Radioactive Dating.* San Diego: Institute for Creation Research, 1973.

Smith, David W. "Compendium of Shortness of Stature." *Journal of Pediatrics,* Vol. 70, March 1967.

Smith, Hilton A., and Jones, Thomas C. *Veterinary Pathology.* Third edition. Philadelphia: Lea & Febiger, 1966.

Standen, Anthony. *Science Is a Sacred Cow.* New York: E. P. Dutton, 1950.

Storer, Tracy I.; Usinger, Robert L.; Stebbins, Robert C.; and Nybakken, James W. *General Zoology.* Fifth edition. New York: McGraw-Hill Book Company, 1972.

Strauss, Maurice, and Welt, Louis G. *Diseases of the Kidney.* Third edition. Boston: Little, Brown & Company, 1963.

Takeuchi, H., Uyeda, S., and Kanamori, H. *Debate About the Earth.* San Francisco: Freeman, Cooper, & Company, 1970.

Tanner, J. M.; Prader, A.; Habich, H.; and Ferguson-Smith, M. A. "Genes on the Y Chromosome Influencing Rate of Maturation in Man." *Lancet,* Vol. 2, 1959.

Tashian, Richard. "Metabolism." *Clinical and Experimental Medicine.* Vol. 10, September 28, 1957, pp. 393-402.

Thorpe, W. H. *Learning and Instinct in Animals.* Cambridge: Harvard University Press, 1963.

Tilton, G. R., and Steiger, R. H. "Lead Isotopes and the Age of the Earth." *Science.* Vol. 150, December 1965.

Urback, Frederick. *The Biologic Effects of Ultraviolet Radiation.* First edition. New York: Pergamon Press, 1969.

Vandeman, George E. *Plant in Rebellion.* Nashville, Tenn.: Southern Publishing Association, 1960.

Van Tyne, Josselyn, and Berger, Andrew J. *Fundamentals of Ornithology.* New York: John Wiley & Sons, 1959.

Wallace, Bruce, and Srb, Adrian M. *Adaptation.* Second edition. Englewood Cliffs, N.J.: Prentice-Hall, 1964.

Warkany, Josef. *Congenital Malformations, Notes and Comments.* Chicago: Year Book Medical Publishers, 1971.

Weiss, Eric A., editor. *Computer Usage Fundamentals of the Computer Usage Company.* New York: McGraw-Hill Book Company, 1969.

Welch, Claude A., et al. *Biological Science: Molecules to Man.* Boston: Houghton Mifflin, 1968.

Whitcomb, John C., and Morris, Henry M. *The Genesis Flood.* Philadelphia: Presbyterian and Reformed Publishing Company, 1965.

White, E. G. *Patriarchs and Prophets.* Mountain View, Calif.: Pacific Press Publishing Association, 1913.

Williams, Marian, and Lissner, Herbert R. *Biomechanics of Human Motion.* Philadelphia: W. B. Saunders Company, 1962.

Willis, R. A. *The Borderland of Embryology and Pathology.* Washington, D.C.: Butterworthe, 1967.

World Book Encyclopedia. Vols. B2, D5. Chicago: Field Enterprises Educational Corporation, 1968.

Index

Mental deterioration, 144, 145
Mental retardation, 132-33, 141, 153-54
Metabolism, 81-83, 121; PKU an inherited error of, 131, 132, 133
Microcephaly, 55-57, 126
Midgets, 143, 144
Missing links, 51, 57-59
Molecular Insights into Living Processes, 49-50
Mongolism. *See* Down's Syndrome
More, Louis, 16
Moses, 17, 19, 157, 160
Motion, 94-103; birds, 100-03; cerebellum, role of, 97-98; hands, 98-100; normal walking, 94-95; running, 97
Muller, Fritz, 181
Muscles, 95, 98-99, 109, 117, 118; Muscular Dystrophy, 135-37
Muscular Dystrophy, 135-37; Duchenne type, 135, 155; muscular degeneration, 135-36; types of, 135

National Aeronautics and Space Administration (NASA), 78-79, 171
Nature (magazine), 50
Nervous system, 97, 100, 109, 110, 114, 145; autonomic, 64; central, 75, 76, 80, 159; sympathetic, 174
Noachian Deluge, 160-61, 165. *See also* Flood

Oddi, sphincter of, 89
Origin of the Species by Means of Natural Selection, The, 58
Osborn, Dr. Henry Fairfield, 26
Oxygen, 67, 80-81, 120, 133, 137

Pancreas, 62, 87, 146
Pascal's Law, 119
Pelvis, 95, 175
Penguins, 180
Phagocytes, 109, 110
Phenylalanine, 132, 133
Phenyketonuria (PKU), 131-33; associated defects, 133; bio-

chemical explanation for, 132, 133; incidence of, 133; medical recognition of, 132; mental retardation, a cause of, 132, 133; prevention of, 133
Pigmentation, 178; skin, 91-92, 174, 177
Pituitary gland, 85, 143-44; anterior, 70; posterior, 68-69
PKU. *See* Phenylketonuria
Polycystic kidney disease, 145-46; adult form, 146; neonatal form, 145-46
Polydactyly, 147-48
Progeria (Hutchinson-Gilford Syndrome), 123
Proteins, 81-83, 87, 109, 141; hemoglobin, 80-81; insulin, 61-62; synthesis of, 60-61
Prothrombin, 88, 104, 105
Purkinje system, 85
Pygmies, 143-44
Pyloric stenosis, 150

Q-values, 165, 166

Radioactive decay, 164, 167
Recapitulation, Theory of, 180-83
Reflexes; 73; coughing, 117, 176; protection mechanisms, 114-15, 117-18; vomiting, 117-18
Respiration, 64-68, 77; acid-base regulation, 77; chemoreceptors, 65-67; expiration, 65; inspiration, 65; rate of, 65
Ribonucleic acid (RNA), 61, 62

Safety margins, Creator-designed, 176-77
Scar tissue, 109-10
Scopes, John T., 24-26, 27
Scopes trial, 24-27
Sex chromosomal abnormalities, 150-55; hermaphrodites, true, 151, 155; Klinefelter's Syndrome, 153, 154, 155; triple-X females, 154; Turner's Syndrome, 151-52, 154, 155; X chromosome, 154-55; XYY (super male) syndrome, 153-54